Wonderful Standards

ISBN 0-634-06965-9

HAL•LEONARD®
CORPORATION

7777 W. BLUEMOUND RD. P.O. BOX 13819 MILWAUKEE, WI 53213

Visit Hal Leonard Online at
www.halleonard.com

CONTENTS

4	After You've Gone
7	Ain't Misbehavin'
10	Autumn Leaves
16	Bluesette
13	Body and Soul
20	Dinah
23	The Girl from Ipanema (Garôta de Ipanema)
26	Honeysuckle Rose
29	How Deep Is the Ocean (How High Is the Sky)
32	How High the Moon
35	How Insensitive (Insensatez)
38	I Gotta Right to Sing the Blues
44	I Should Care
41	I've Got the World on a String
46	I've Got You Under My Skin
50	I've Grown Accustomed to Her Face
53	My Favorite Things
56	My Romance
58	Red Roses for a Blue Lady
64	September Song
66	Slightly Out of Tune (Desafinado)
61	Some Enchanted Evening
70	So Nice (Summer Samba)
72	Watch What Happens
75	Younger Than Springtime

After You've Gone

from ONE MO' TIME

Electronic Organs
Upper: Flutes (or Tibias) 16', 8', 4'
Lower: Melodia 8', Reed 8'
Pedal: 8'
Vib./Trem.: On, Fast
Rhythm: Fox Trot or Swing

Drawbar Organs
Upper: 80 4800 000
Lower: (00) 7334 011
Pedal: 05
Vib./Trem.: On, Fast
Rhythm: Fox Trot or Swing

Words by Henry Creamer
Music by Turner Layton

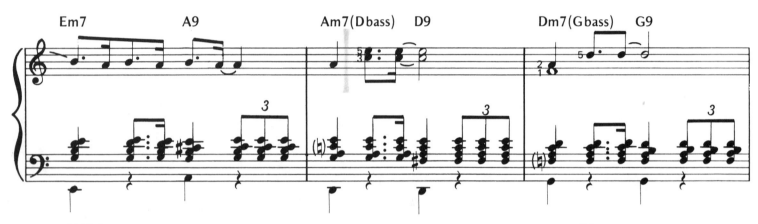

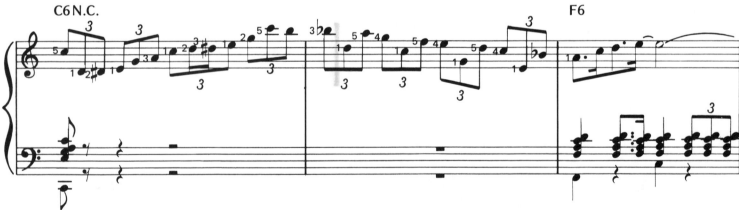

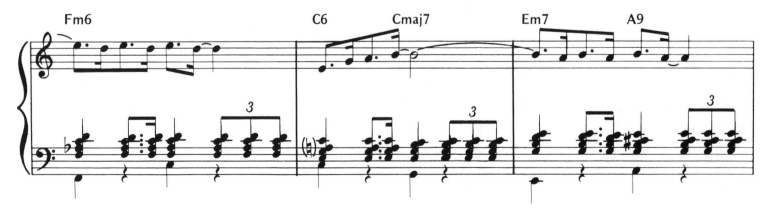

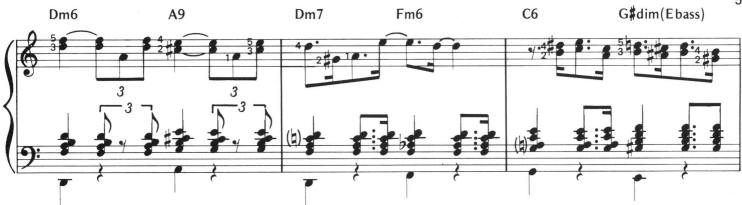

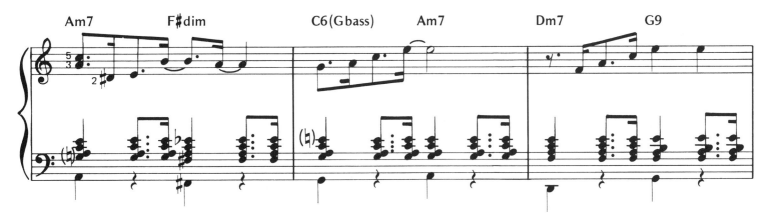

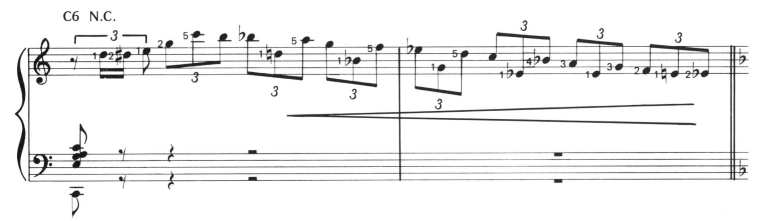

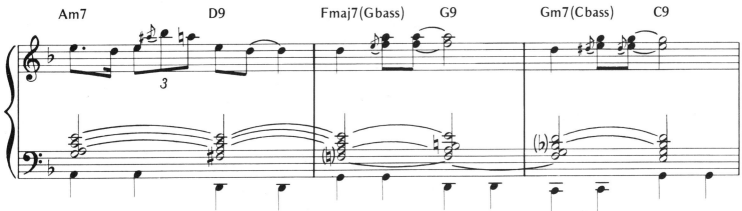

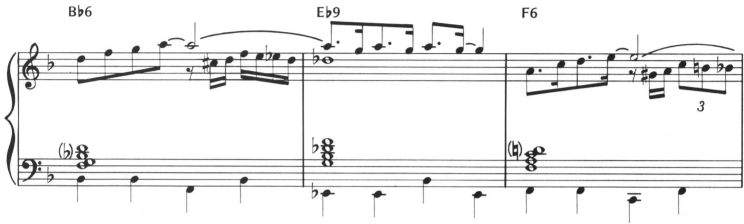

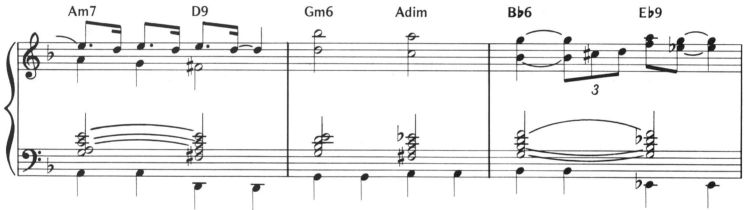

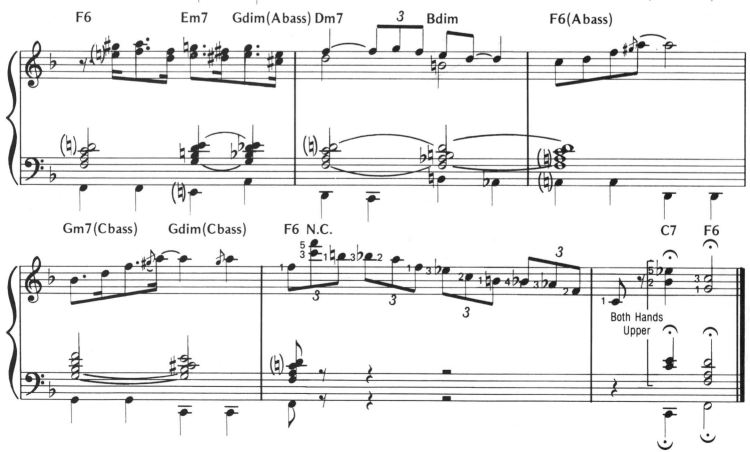

Ain't Misbehavin'

from AIN'T MISBEHAVIN'

Electronic Organs
Upper: Flutes (or Tibias) 16′, 8′, 5⅓′, 4′, 2′
Lower: Flute 4′, Diapason 8′
Pedal: String Bass
Vib./Trem.: On, Slow

Tonebar Organs
Upper: 85 0000 355
Lower: (00) 8401 007
Pedal: String Bass
Vib./Trem.: On, Slow

Words by Andy Razaf
Music by Thomas "Fats" Waller and Harry Brooks

8

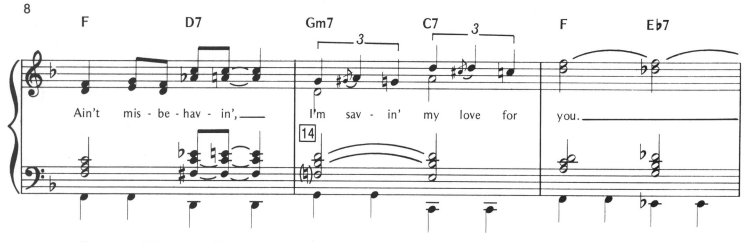

Ain't mis-be-hav-in', ___ I'm sav-in' my love for you. ___

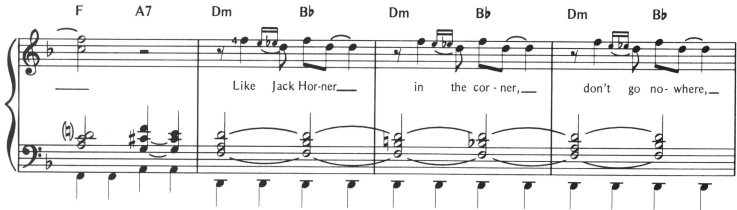

Like Jack Hor-ner ___ in the cor-ner, ___ don't go no-where, ___

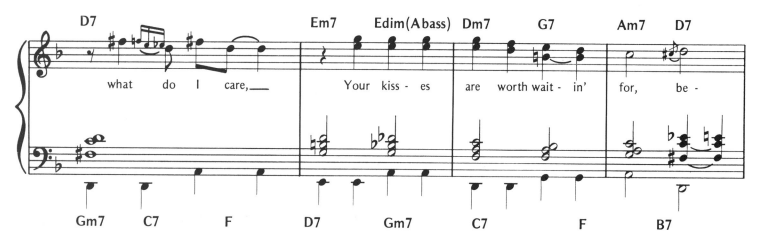

what do I care, ___ Your kiss-es are worth wait-in' for, be-

lieve me I don't stay out late, don't care to go, ___ I'm home a-bout eight, just

me and my ra-di-o, ___ Ain't mis-be-hav-in' I'm sav-in' my love for

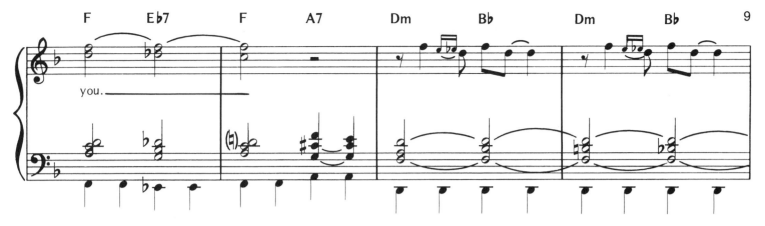

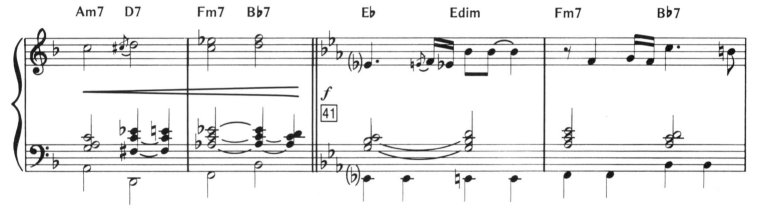

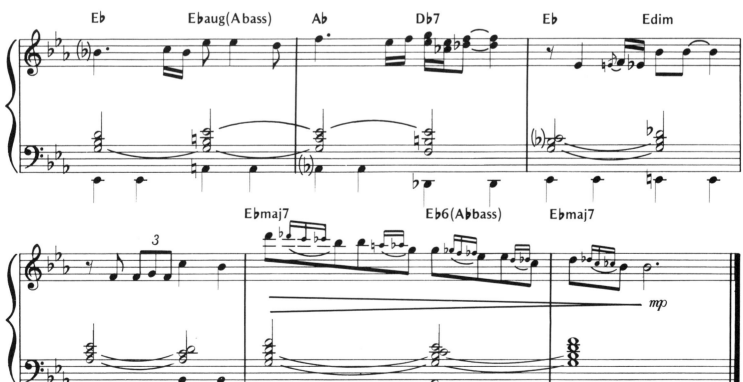

Autumn Leaves

Electronic Organs
Upper: Flutes (or Tibias) 16', 4'
       String 8'
Lower: Flutes 8', 4', Diapason 8'
Pedal: String Bass
Vib./Trem.: On, Fast
Rhythm: Ballad or Fox Trot

Drawbar Organs
Upper: 60 3616 113
Lower: (00) 7634 212
Pedal: String Bass
Vib./Trem.: On, Fast
Rhythm: Ballad or Fox Trot

English lyric by Johnny Mercer
French lyric by Jacques Prevert
Music by Joseph Kosma

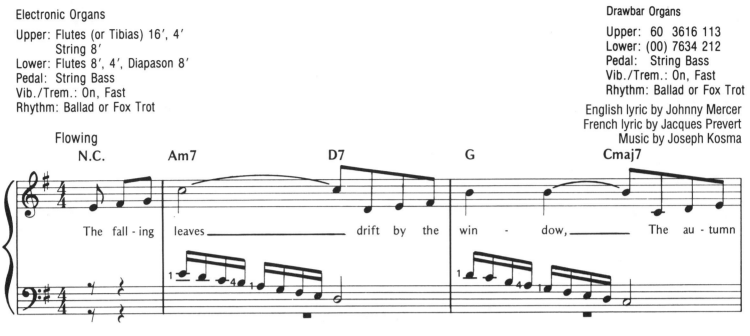

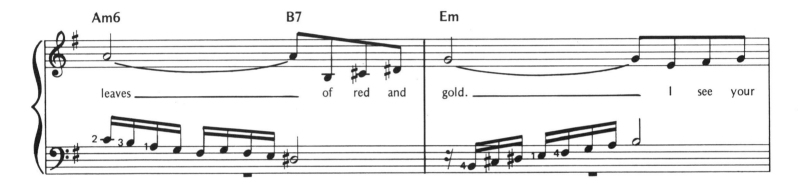

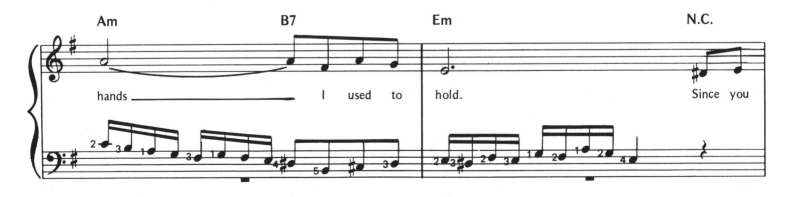

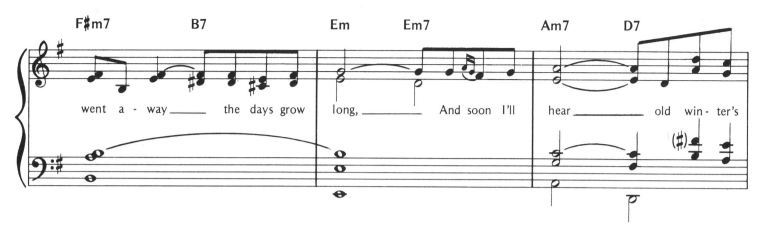

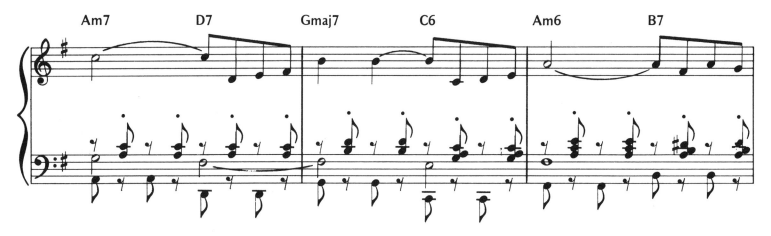

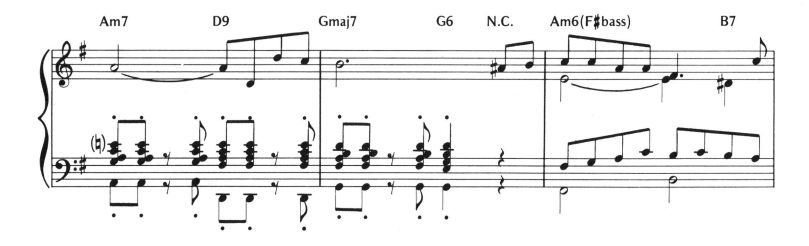

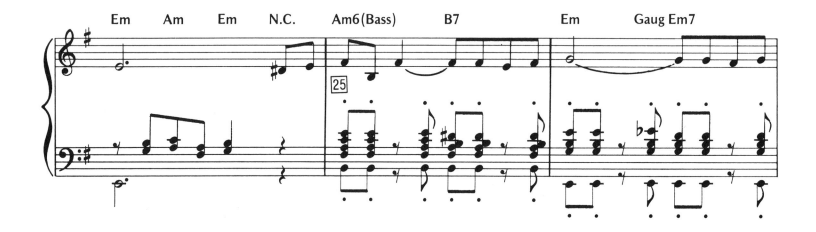

Body and Soul

Electronic Organs

Upper: Saxophone 16', or Trombone 16'
Cello 16'
Lower: Flutes 8', 4', Strings 8', 4'
Pedal: 8' Sustain
Vib/Trem: On — Full
Automatic Rhythm: Swing (optional)

Drawbar Organs

Upper: 85 8533 522 (00)
Lower: (00) 5743 332 (0)
Pedal: 4 (0) 6 (0) (Spinet 5)
Vib/Trem: On — Full
Automatic Rhythm: Swing (optional)

Words by Edward Heyman,
Robert Sour and Frank Eyton
Music by John Green

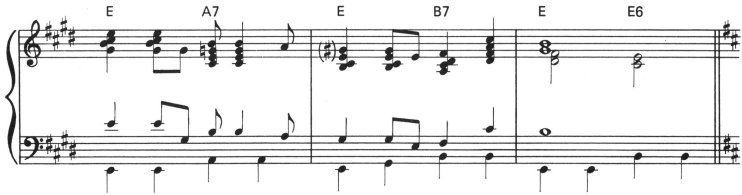

Bluesette

Electronic Organs

Upper: Flutes (or Tibias) 16', 4', 2'
Lower: Flutes 8', 4'
Pedal: 8' Sustain
Vib/Trem: On — Full

Drawbar Organs

Upper: 80 0808 530 (00)
Lower: (00) 6533 322 (0)
Pedal: 5 (0) 4 (0) (Spinet 5)
String Bass
Vib/Trem: On — Full

Words by Norman Gimbel
Music by Jean Thielemans

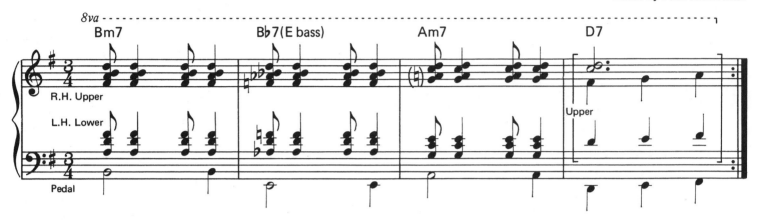

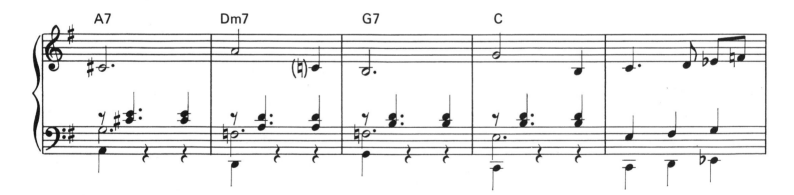

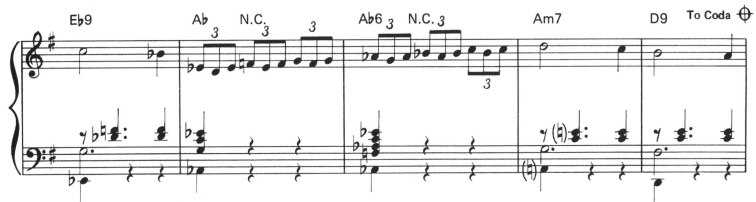

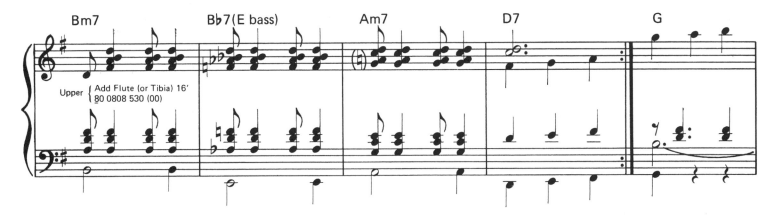

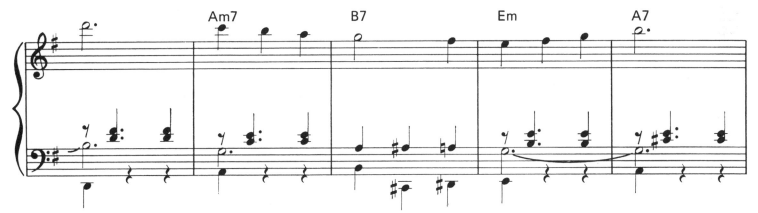

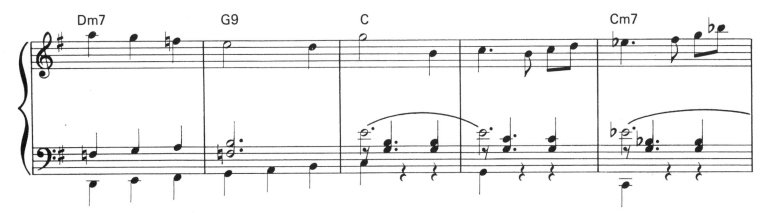

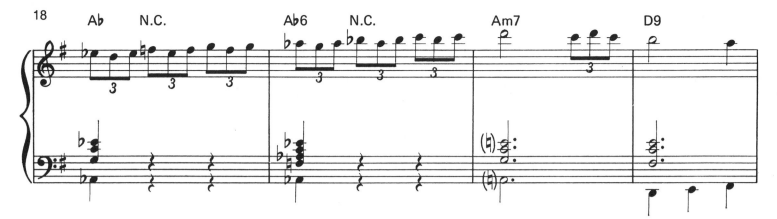

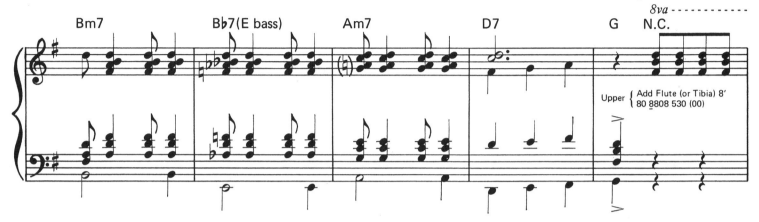

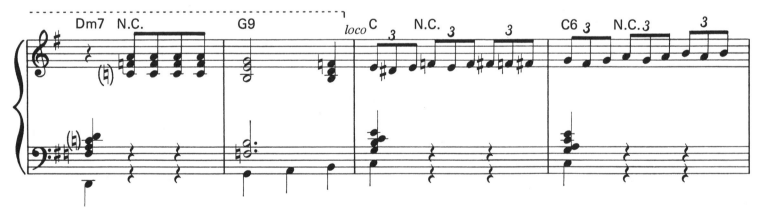

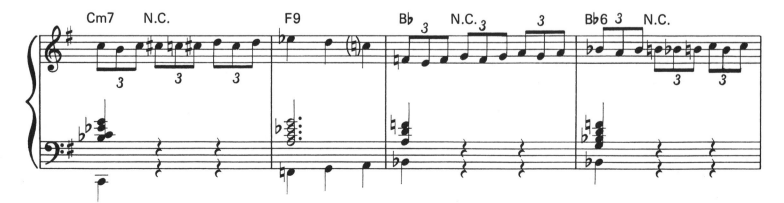

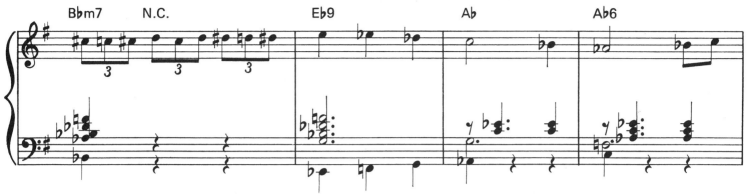

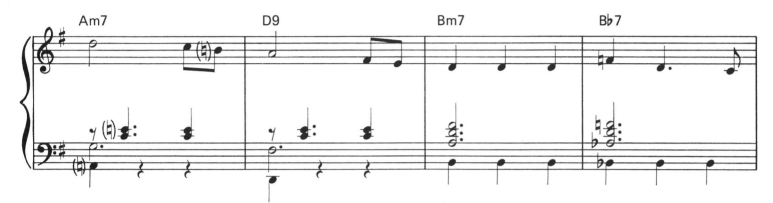

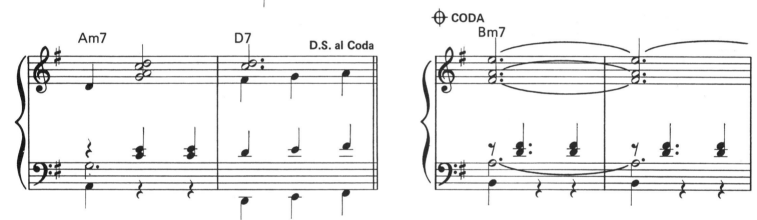

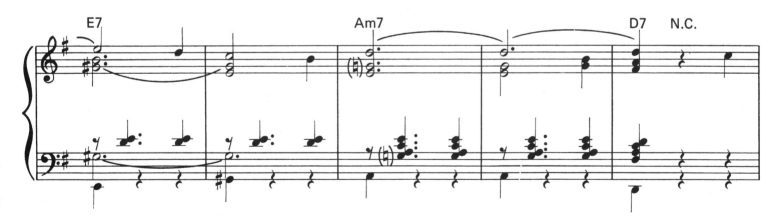

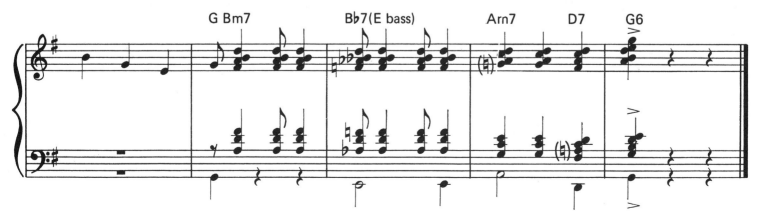

Dinah
from THE BIG BROADCAST

Electronic Organs
Upper: Flutes (or Tibias) 16′, 8′, 5⅓′, 4′
Lower: Flute 4′, Diapason 8′
Pedal: String Bass
Vib./Trem.: On, Slow

Drawbar Organs
Upper: 85 0000 350
Lower: (00) 8401 007
Pedal: String Bass
Vib./Trem.: On, Slow

Words by Sam M. Lewis and Joe Young
Music by Harry Akst

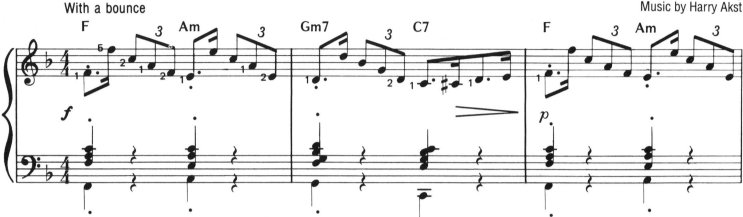

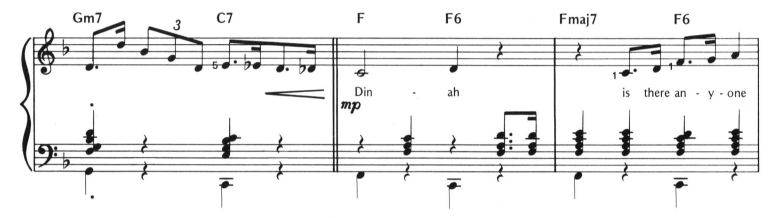

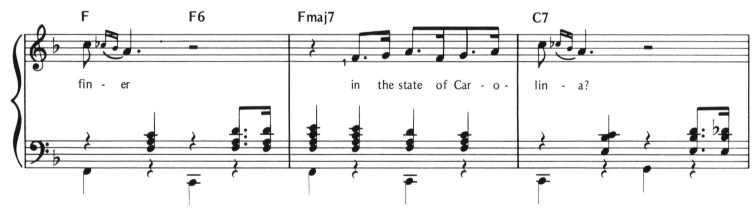

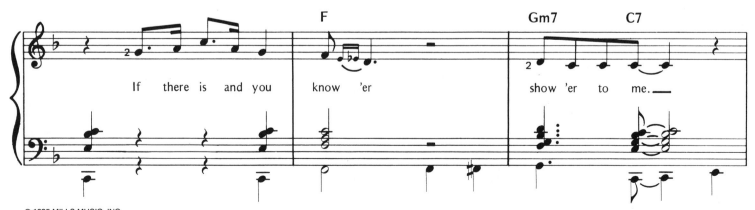

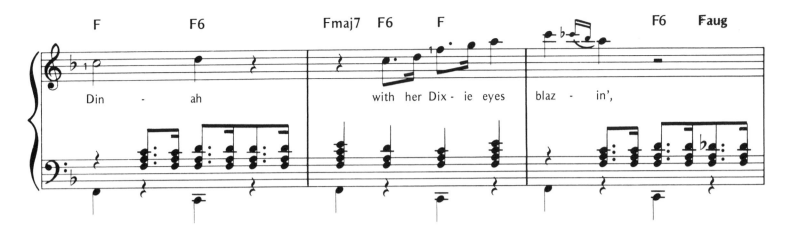

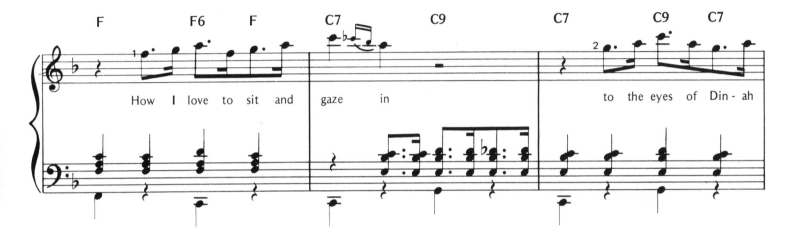

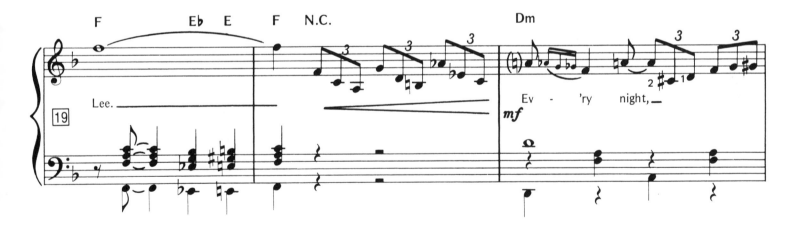

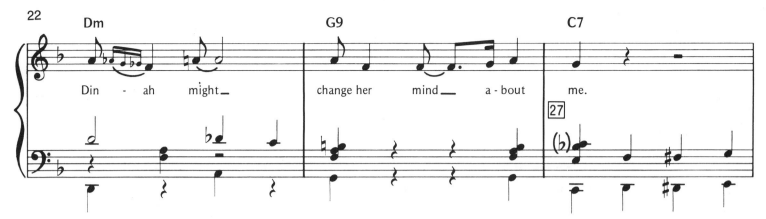

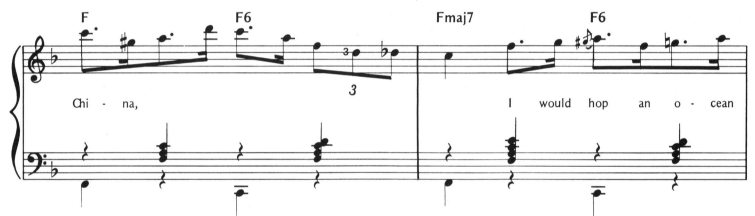

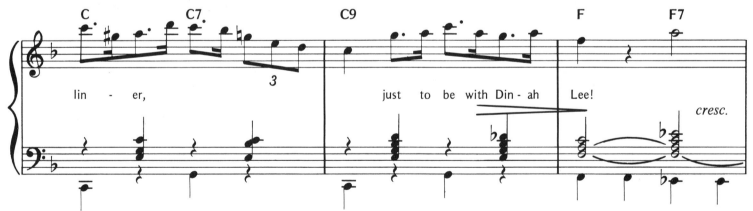

The Girl from Ipanema
(Garôta de Ipanema)

Electronic Organs
Upper: Flutes (or Tibias) 16′, 8′, 4′
Lower: Melodia 8′, Reed 8′
Pedal: 8′
Vib./Trem.: On, Fast

Drawbar Organs
Upper: 80 4800 000
Lower: (00) 7334 011
Pedal: 05
Vib./Trem.: On, Fast

Music by Antonio Carlos Jobim
English Words by Norman Gimbel
Original Words by Vinicius de Moraes

Tall and tan and young___ and love - ly, the girl from I - pa - ne -
When she walks she's like___ a sam - ba that swings so cool and sways___

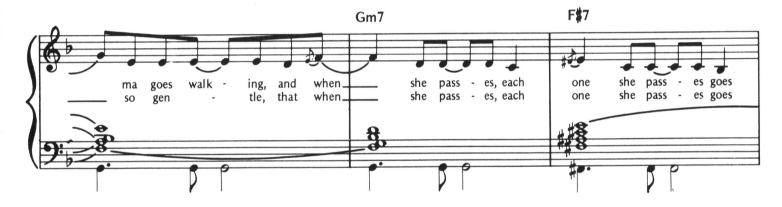

ma goes walk - ing, and when___ she pass - es, each one she pass - es goes
so gen - tle, that when___ she pass - es, each one she pass - es goes

"aah!"   "aah!"

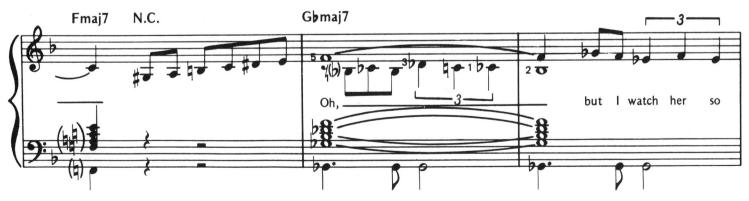

Oh,___   but I watch her so

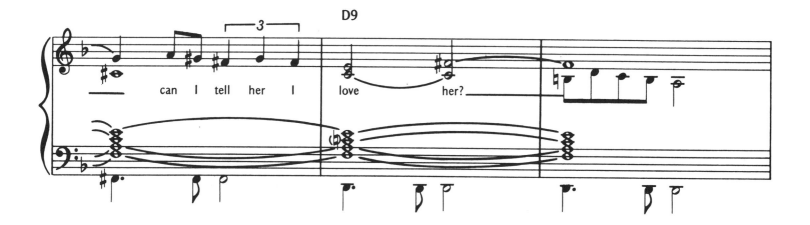

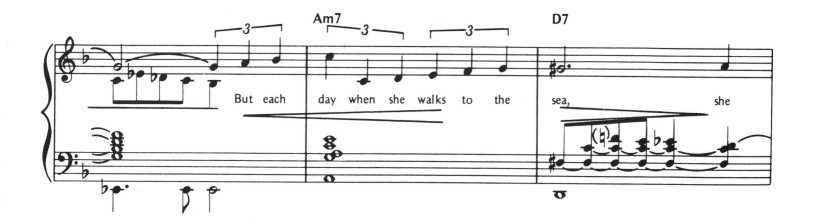

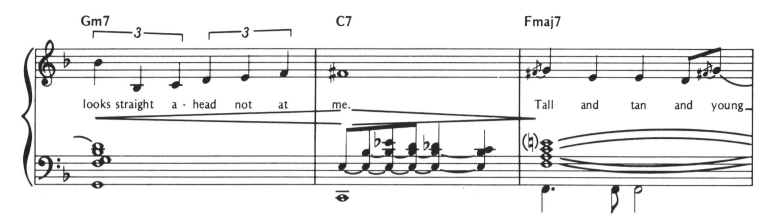

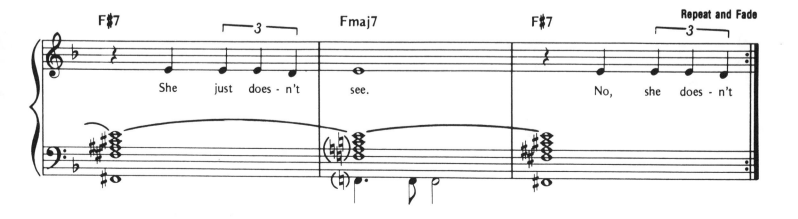

Honeysuckle Rose

from AIN'T MISBEHAVIN'
from TIN PAN ALLEY

Electronic Organs

Upper: Flutes (or Tibias) 16', 4', Clarinet
Lower: Flute 8', 4', Reed 8'
Pedal: 16', 8'
Vib./Trem.: On, Fast

Tonebar Organs

Upper: 82 4203 036
Lower: (00) 6303 003
Pedal: 45
Vib./Trem.: On, Fast

Words by Andy Razaf
Music by Thomas "Fats" Waller

Moderately, with a lilt

Lyrics:
Ev-'ry hon-ey-bee fills with jeal-ous-y when they see you out with me, I don't blame them, good-ness knows, Hon-ey-suck-le Rose.

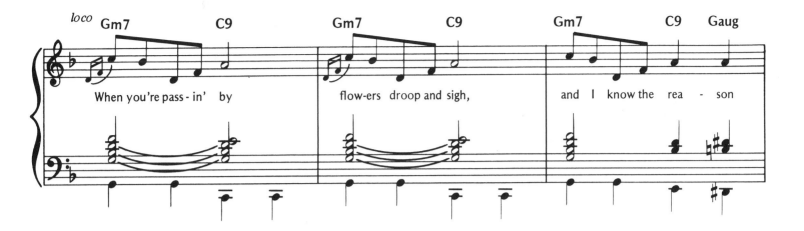

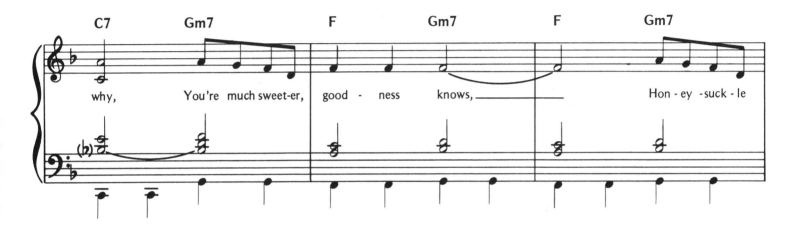

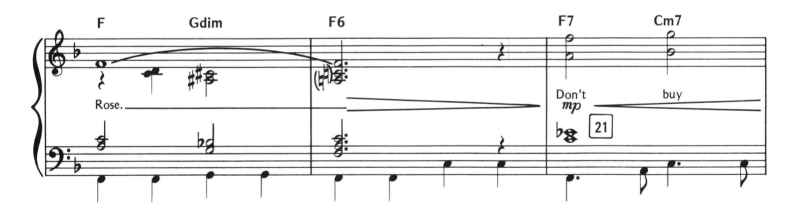

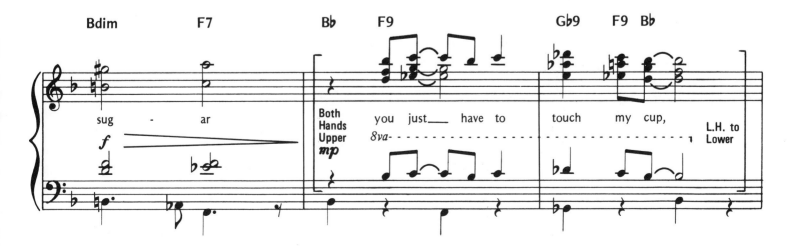

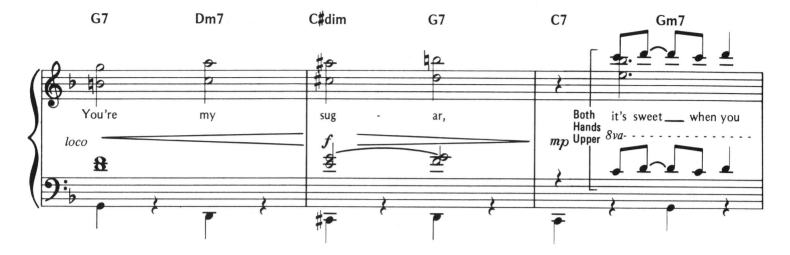

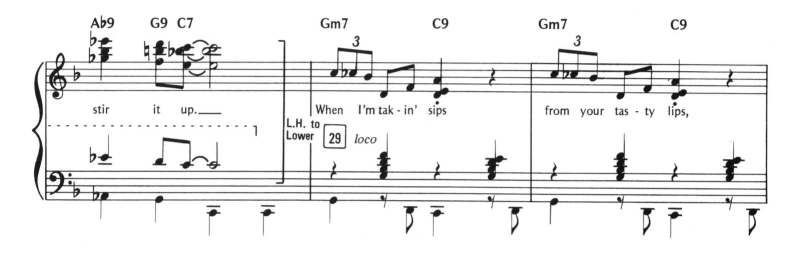

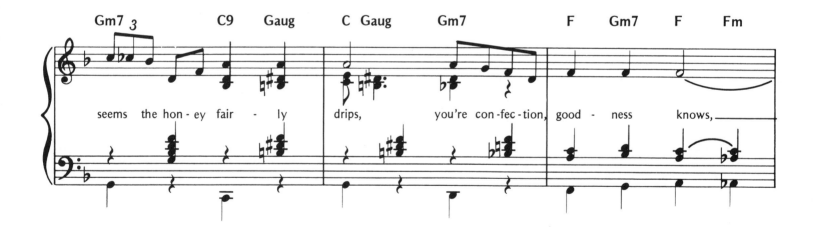

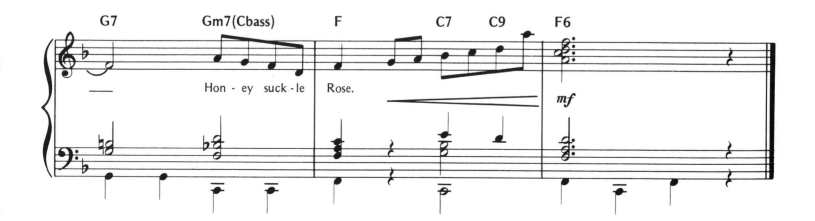

How Deep Is the Ocean

(How High Is the Sky)

Electronic Organs
Upper: Flutes (or Tibias) 16′, 4′
Lower: Flute 8′, Reed
Pedal: 8′, String Bass
Vib./Trem.: On, Fast

Tonebar Organs
Upper: 80 0800 000
Lower: (00) 6500 000
Pedal: 05, String Bass
Vib./Trem.: On, Fast

Words and Music by
Irving Berlin

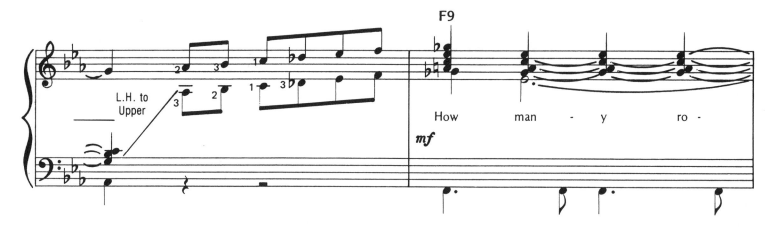

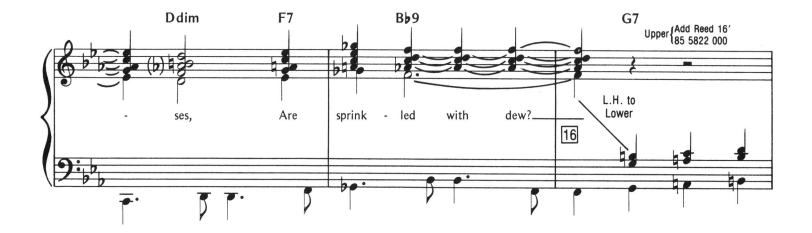

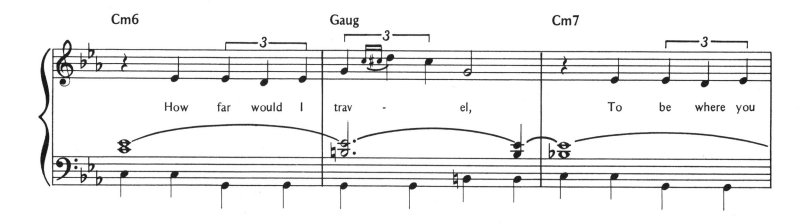

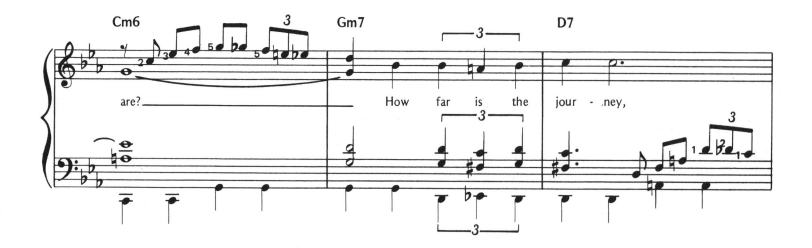

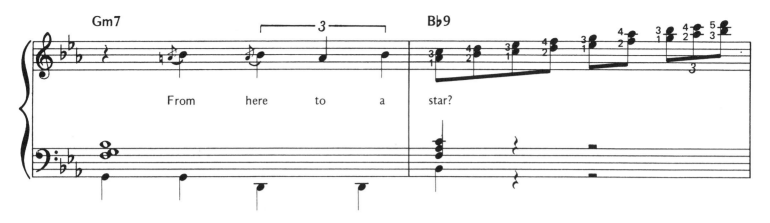

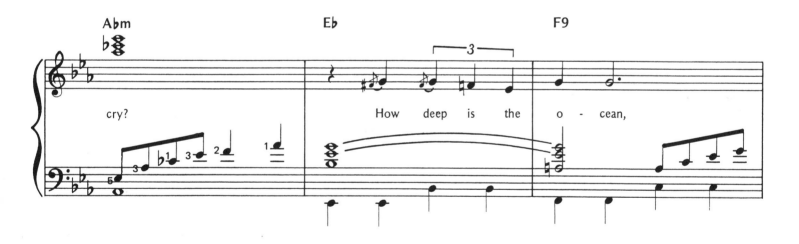

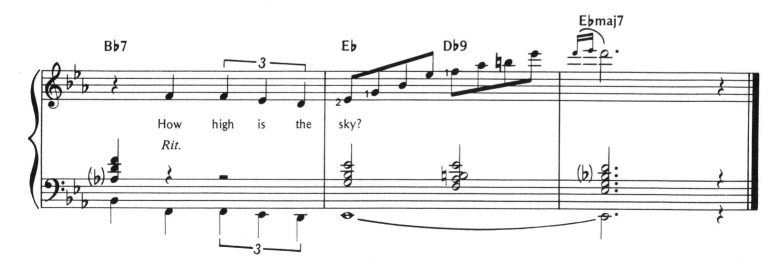

How High the Moon

from TWO FOR THE SHOW

Electronic Organs
Upper: Flutes (or Tibias) 16′, 8′, 5⅓′, 4′, 2′
Lower: Flute 4′, Diapason 8′
Pedal: String Bass
Vib./Trem.: On, Slow

Drawbar Organs
Upper: 85 0000 355
Lower: (00) 8401 007
Pedal: String Bass
Vib./Trem.: On, Slow

Words by Nancy Hamilton
Music by Morgan Lewis

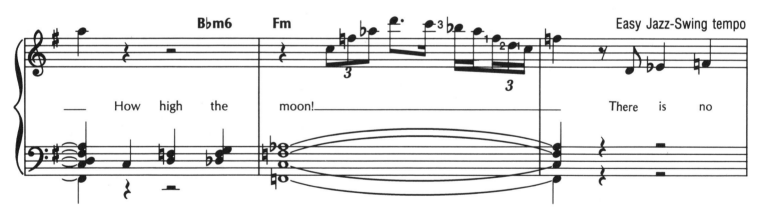

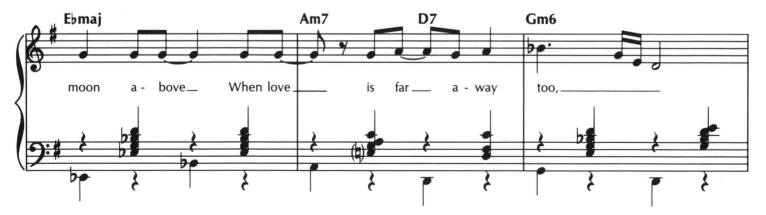

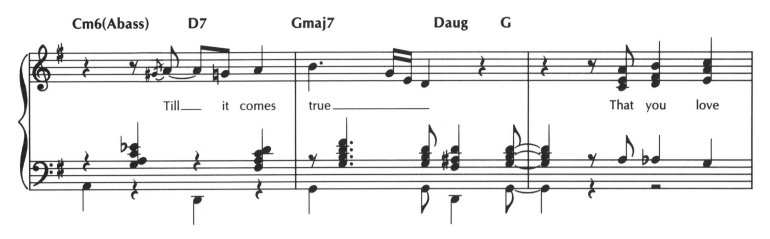

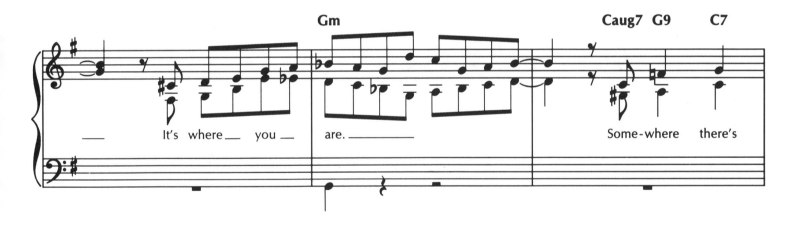

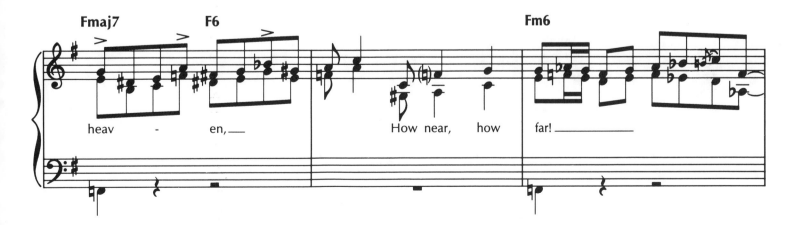

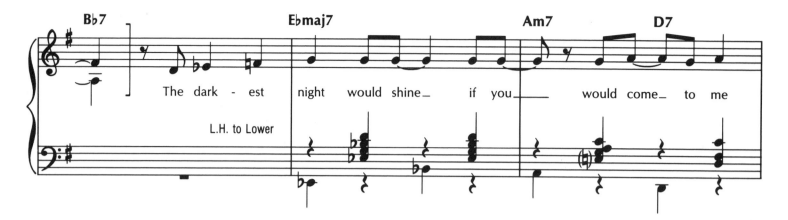

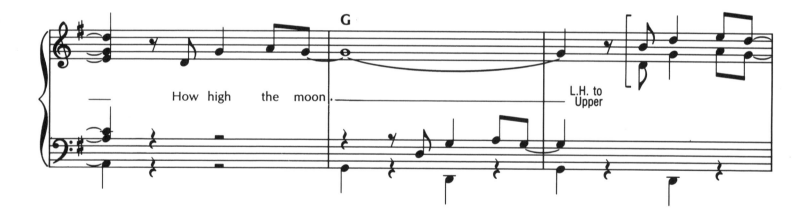

How Insensitive
(Insensatez)

Electronic Organs
Upper: Flutes (or Tibias) 16′, 8′, 4′, 2′
     Strings 8′, 4′
Lower: Flutes 8′, 4′
     Strings 8′, 4′
Pedal: 16′, 8′
Vib./Trem.: On, Fast

Tonebar Organs
Upper: 82 5325 004
Lower: (00) 7345 312
Pedal: 44
Vib./Trem.: On, Fast

Music by Antonio Carlos Jobim
Original Words by Vinicius de Moraes
English Words by Norman Gimbel

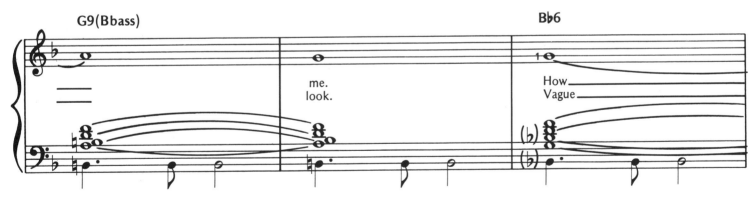

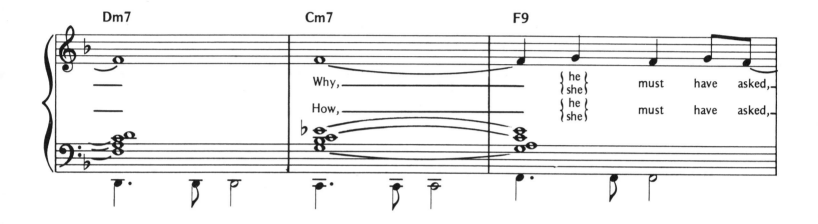

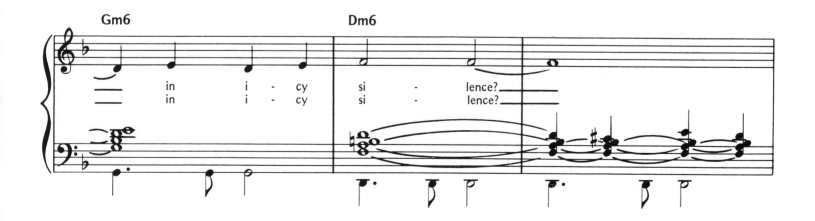

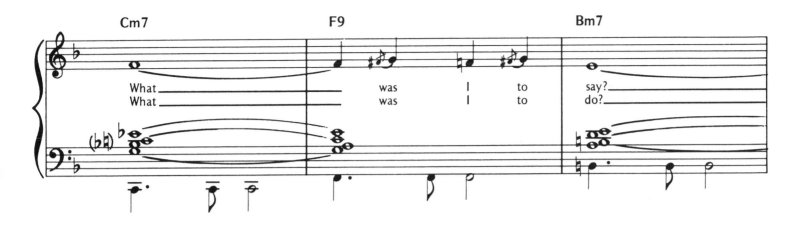

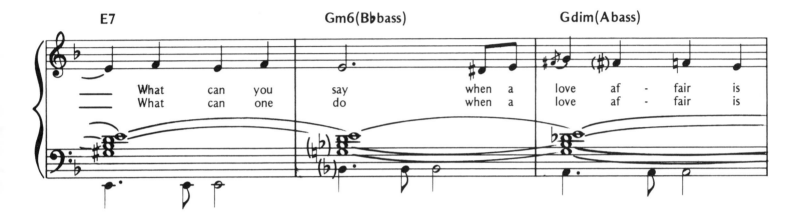

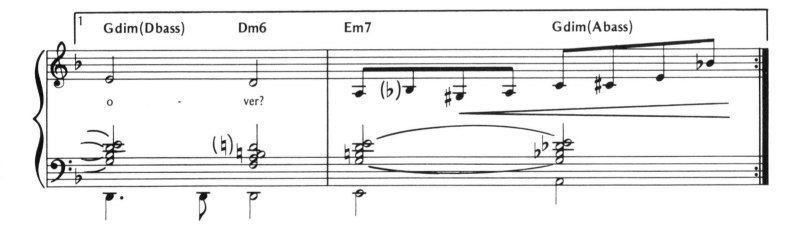

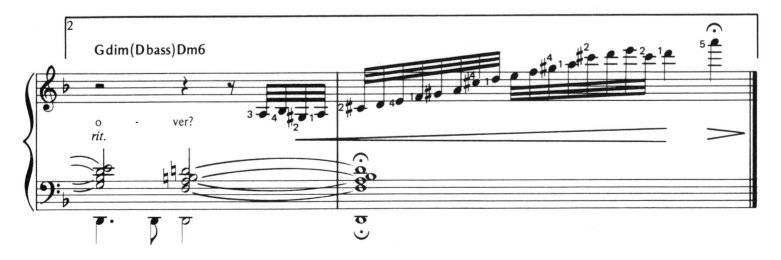

I Gotta Right to Sing the Blues

Electronic Organs

Upper: Clarinet 8'
Lower: Flutes 8', 4', String 8', 4'
Pedal: 8' Sustain
Vib/Trem: On — Full
Automatic Rhythm: Swing

Drawbar Organs

Upper: 00 8060 500 (00)
Lower: (00) 5643 222 (0)
Pedal: 4 (0) 6 (0) (Spinet 5)
         String Bass
Vib/Trem: On — Full
Automatic Rhythm: Swing

Words by Ted Koehler
Music by Harold Arlen

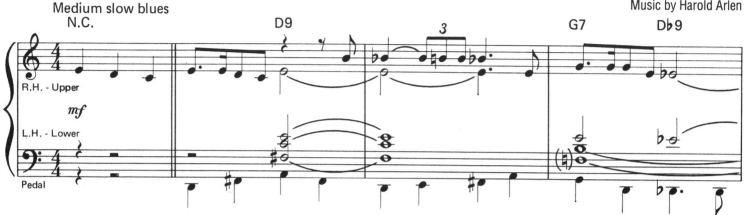

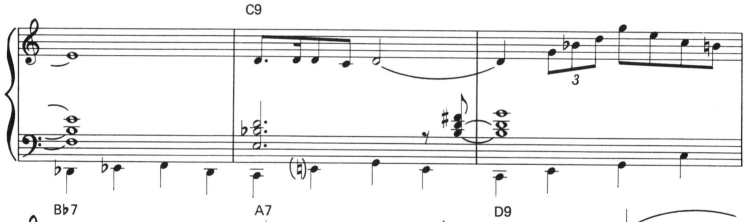

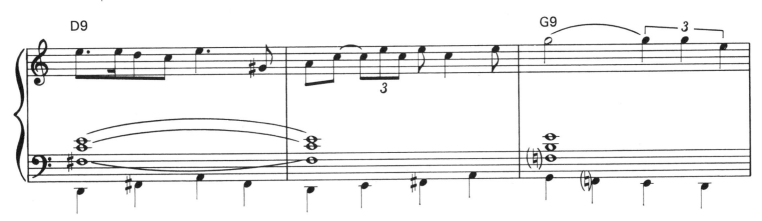

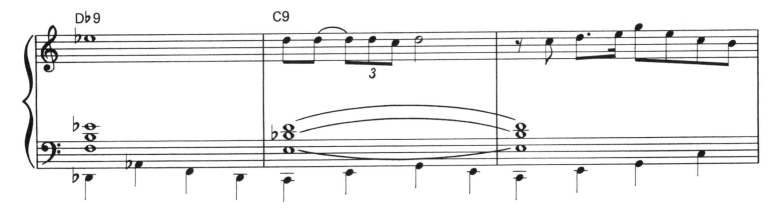

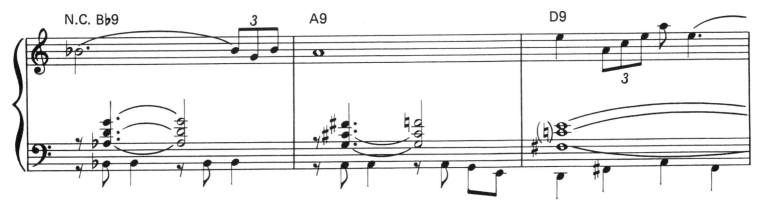

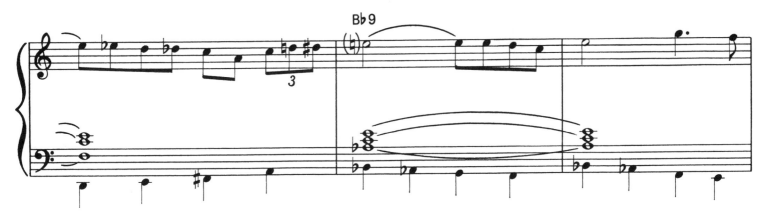

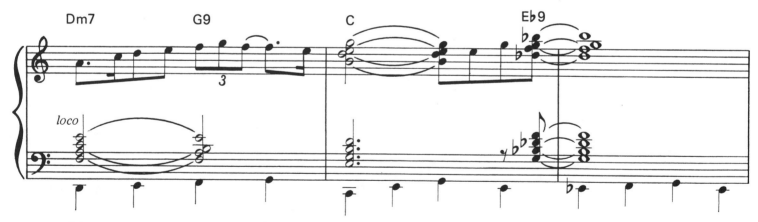

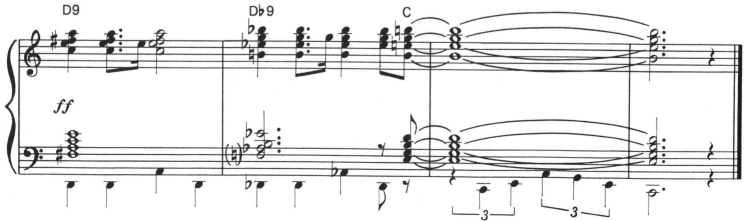

I've Got the World on a String

Electronic Organs

Upper: Flutes (or Tibias) 16', 8', 4',
Lower: Melodia 8', Reed 8'
Pedal: 8'
Vib./Trem.: On, Fast

Tonebar Organs

Upper: 80 4800 000
Lower: (00) 7334 011
Pedal: 05
Vib./Trem.: On, Fast

Lyric by Ted Koehler
Music by Harold Arlen

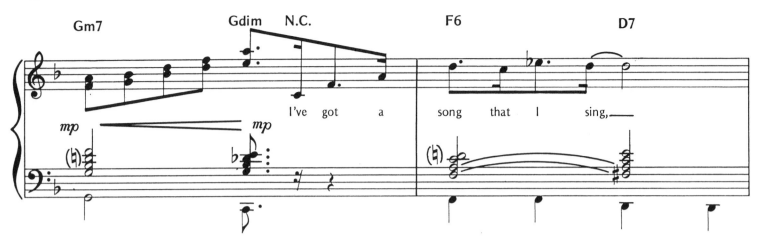

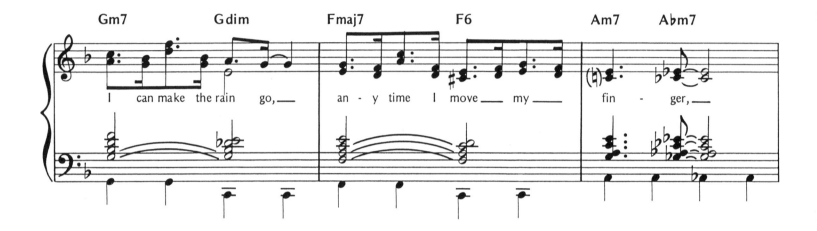

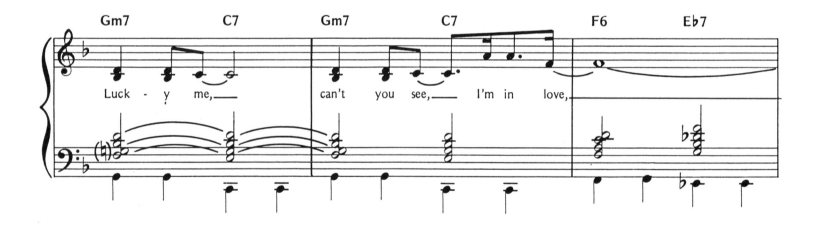

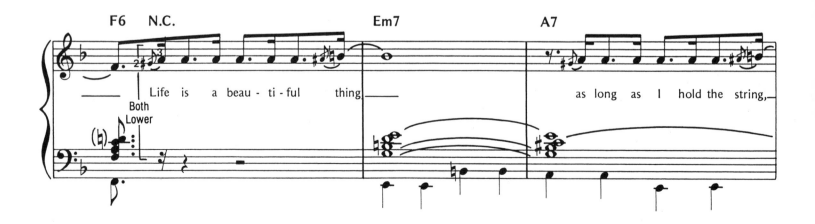

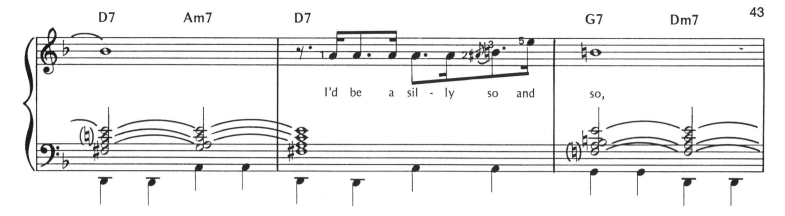

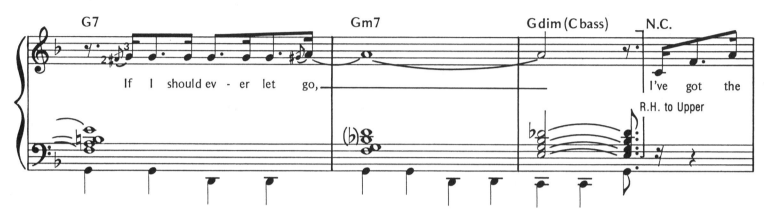

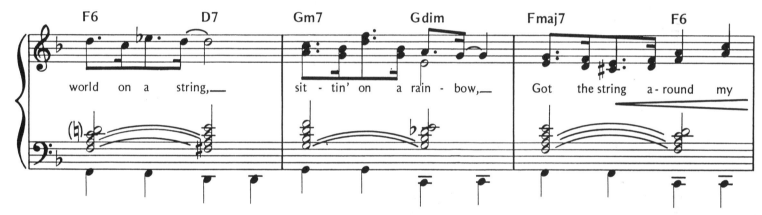

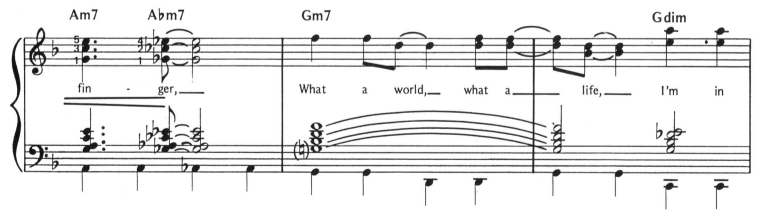

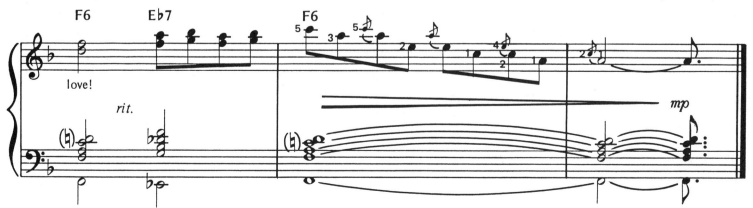

I Should Care

Electronic Organs

Upper: Flutes (or Tibias) 8', 4', 2'
         Strings 8', 4'
Lower: Flutes 8', 4', Reed 4'
Pedal: 16', 8' Sustain
Vib/Trem: On — Full
Automatic Rhythm: Swing/Rhumba

Drawbar Organs

Upper: 00 8848 444 (00)
Lower: (00) 6434 333 (0)
Pedal: 5 (0) 6 (0) (Spinet 5)
       String Bass
Vib/Trem: On — Full
Automatic Rhythm: Swing/Rhumba

Words and Music by Sammy Cahn,
Paul Weston and Axel Stordahl

*Enharmonic — the same key with a different letter name.

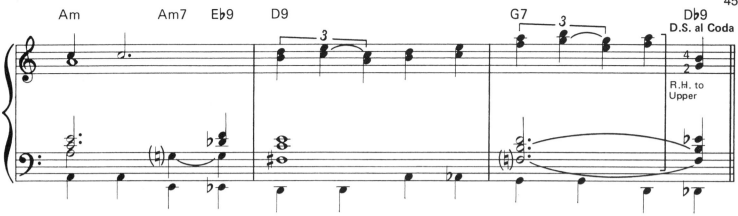

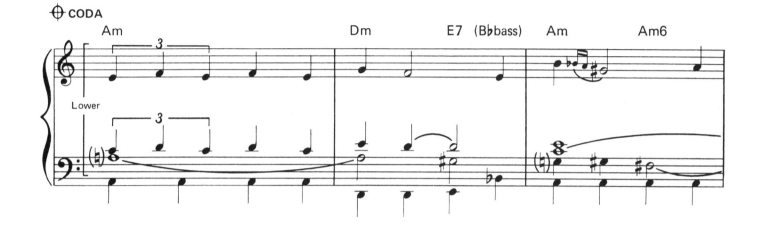

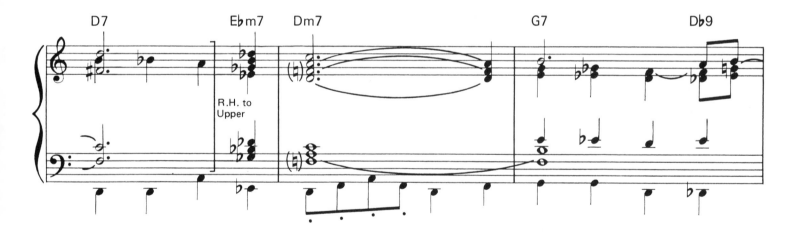

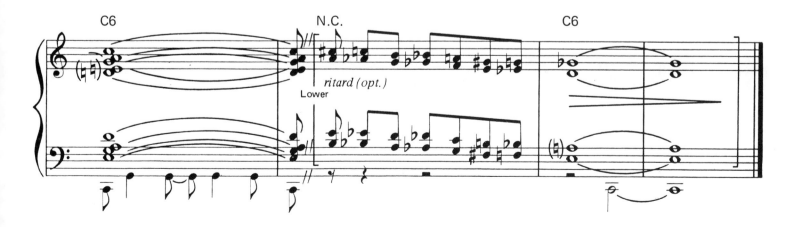

I've Got You Under My Skin

from BORN TO DANCE

Electronic Organs
Upper: Vibes Preset
Lower: Flute (or Tibia) 4', Horn 8'
Pedal: String Bass
Vib./Trem.: On, Slow

Tonebar Organs
Upper: Vibes Preset or
80 0600 100
Sustain, Add Percuss
Lower: (00) 6554 320
Pedal: String Bass
Vib./Trem.: On, Slow

Words and Music by
Cole Porter

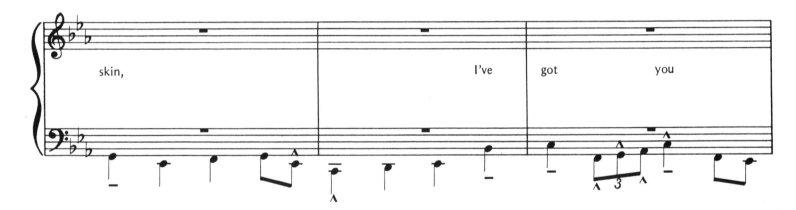

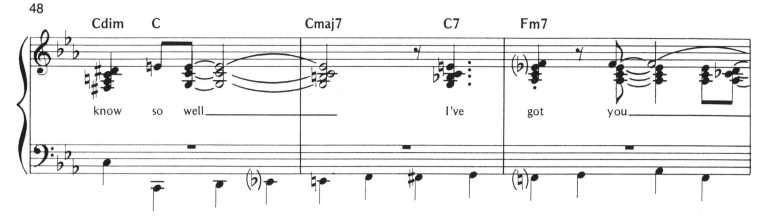

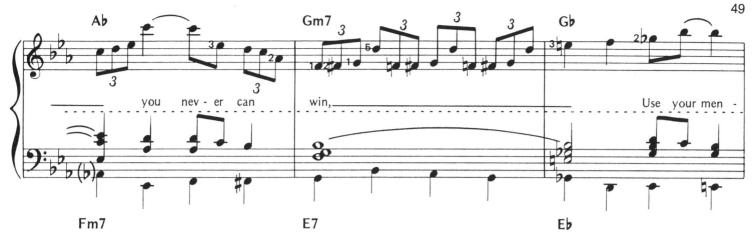

you nev-er can win,_____ Use your men -

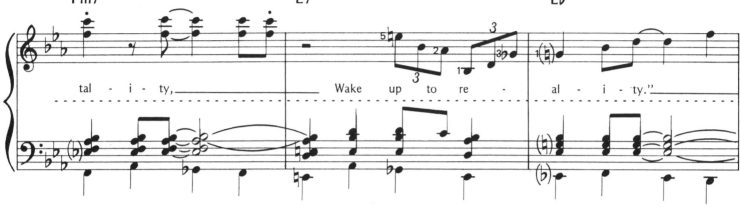

tal - i - ty,_____ Wake up to re - al - i - ty."_____

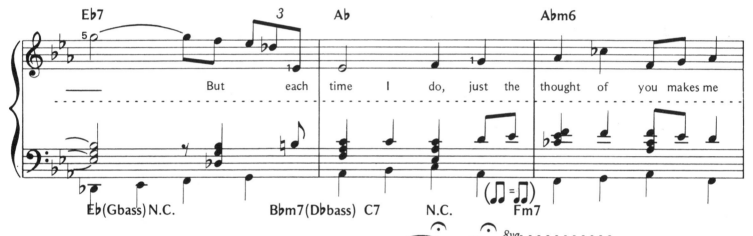

_____ But each time I do, just the thought of you makes me

stop, Be-fore I be-gin, 'Cause I've got you

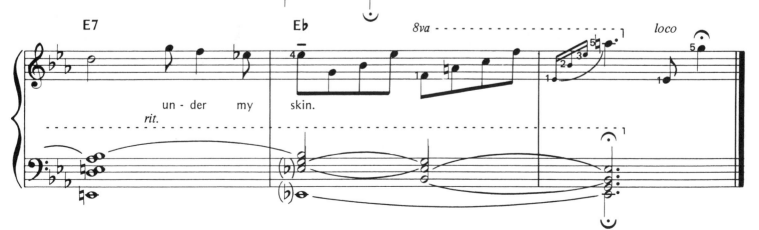

un - der my skin.

I've Grown Accustomed to Her Face

from MY FAIR LADY

Electronic Organs

Upper: Flutes (or Tibias) 16', 8', 4', 2'
       String 8', Clarinet
Lower: Flutes 8', 4'
Pedal: 16', 8'
Vib./Trem.: On, Fast

Tonebar Organs

Upper: 80 8104 103
Lower: (00) 6303 004
Pedal: 35
Vib./Trem.: On, Fast

Words by Alan Jay Lerner
Music by Frederick Loewe

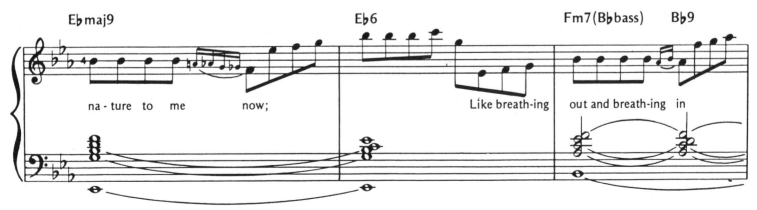

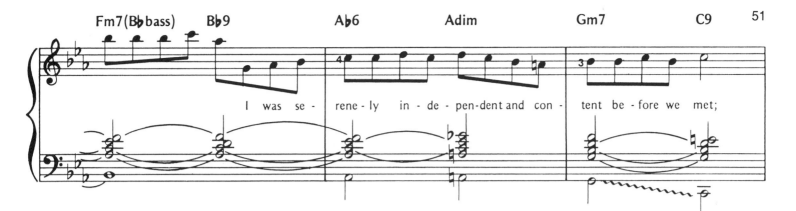

Fm7(B♭bass) B♭9 A♭6 Adim Gm7 C9

I was se-rene-ly in-de-pen-dent and con-tent be-fore we met;

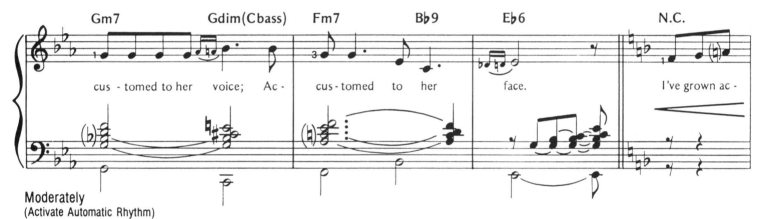

Fm7 B♭9 D♭9(Gbass) C9 N.C. F9(Abass) A♭m6

Sure-ly I could al-ways be that way a-gain and yet, I've grown ac-cus-tomed to her looks; Ac-

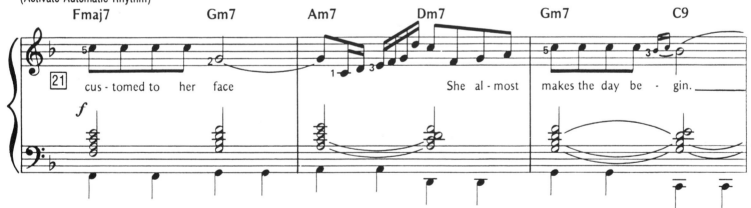

Gm7 Gdim(Cbass) Fm7 B♭9 E♭6 N.C.

cus-tomed to her voice; Ac-cus-tomed to her face. I've grown ac-

Moderately
(Activate Automatic Rhythm)

Fmaj7 Gm7 Am7 Dm7 Gm7 C9

cus-tomed to her face She al-most makes the day be-gin.

f

Gm7 C9 Bb Bdim F6 Am7

I've got-ten used to hear her say: "Good morn-ing" ev-'ry day, Her

cresc.

52

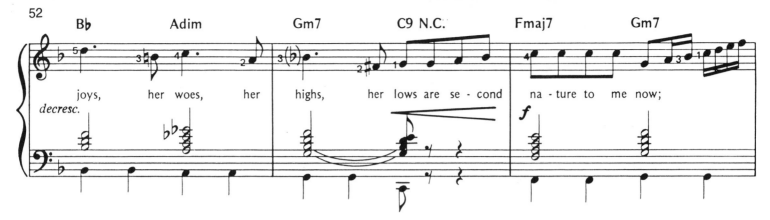

joys, her woes, her highs, her lows are se-cond na-ture to me now;

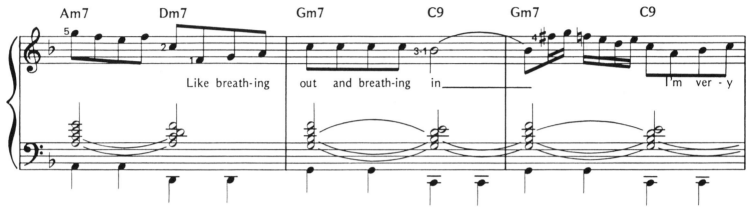

Like breath-ing out and breath-ing in_____ I'm ver-y

grate-ful she's a wo-man and so eas-y to for-get; Rath-er like a ha-bit one can

Ad Lib
(Cancel-Automatic Rhythm)

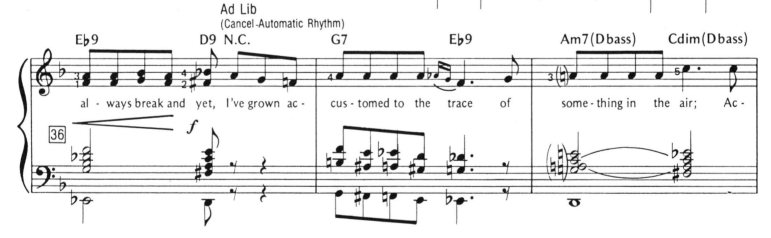

al-ways break and yet, I've grown ac-cus-tomed to the trace of some-thing in the air; Ac-

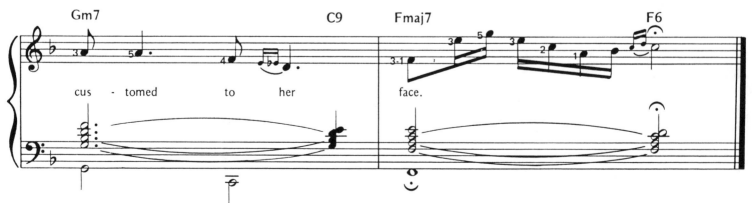

cus-tomed to her face.

My Favorite Things
from THE SOUND OF MUSIC

Electronic Organs
Upper: Flutes (or Tibias) 16′, 8′, 4′,
          Trumpet
Lower: Flutes 8′, 4′, String 8′
Pedal: 16′, 8′
Vib./Trem.: On, Fast

Drawbar Organs
Upper: 80 7766 008
Lower: (00) 8076 000
Pedal: 36
Vib./Trem.: On, Fast

Lyrics by Oscar Hammerstein II
Music by Richard Rodgers

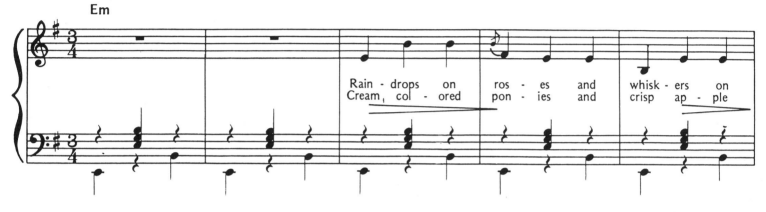

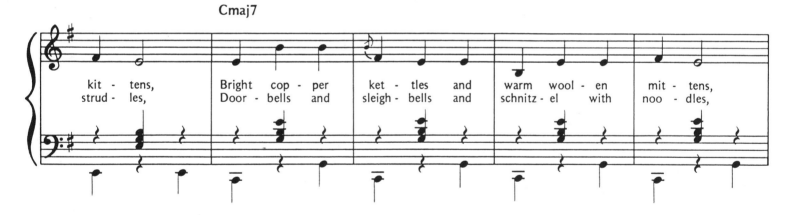

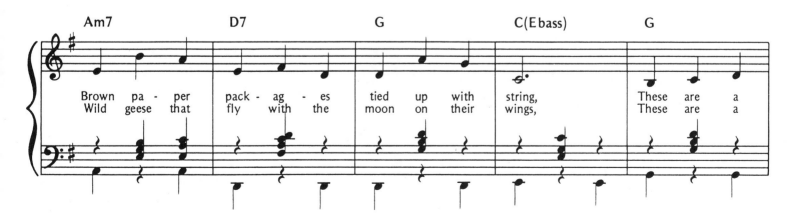

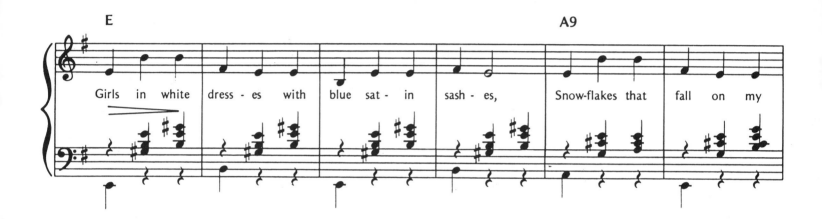

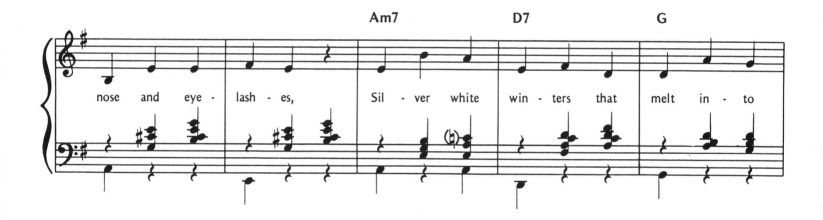

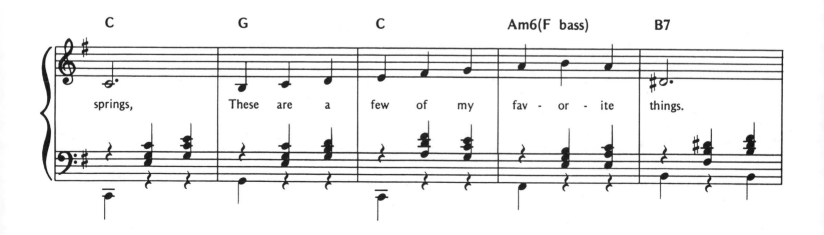

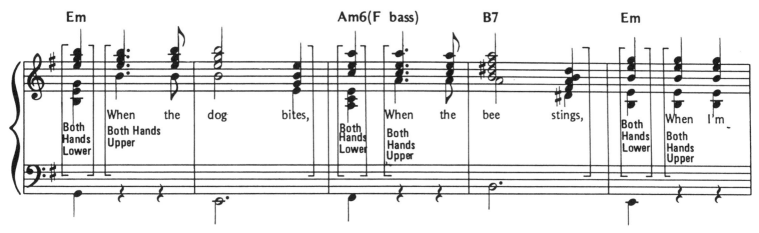

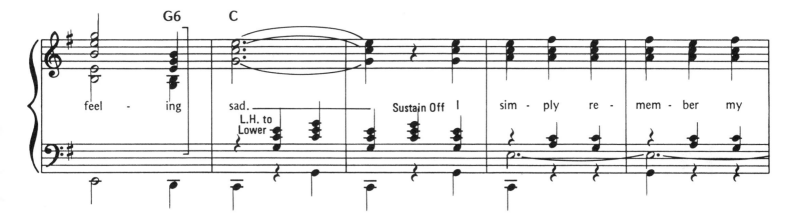

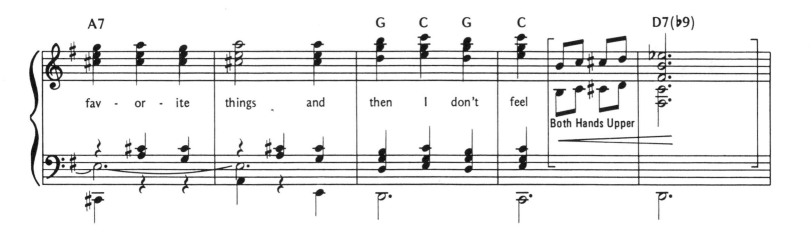

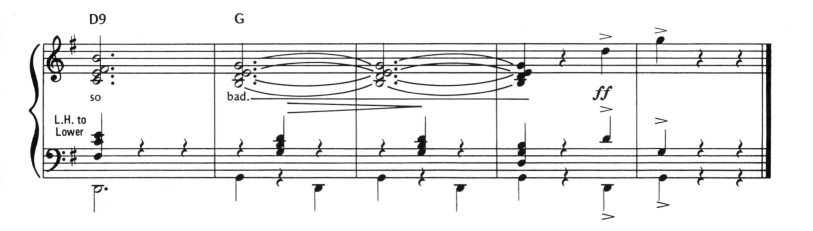

My Romance

from JUMBO

Electronic Organs
Upper: Flute 8′, Clarinet
Lower: Flute 8′, 4′
Pedal: 16′
Vib./Trem.: On, Fast

Tonebar Organs
Upper: 62 3401 021
Lower: (00) 5202 000
Pedal: 43
Vib./Trem.: On, Fast

Words by Lorenz Hart
Music by Richard Rodgers

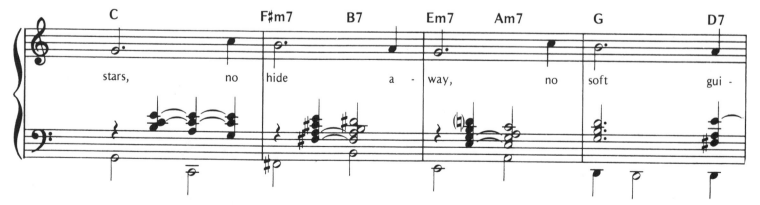

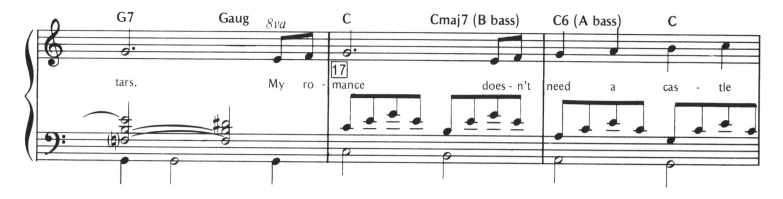

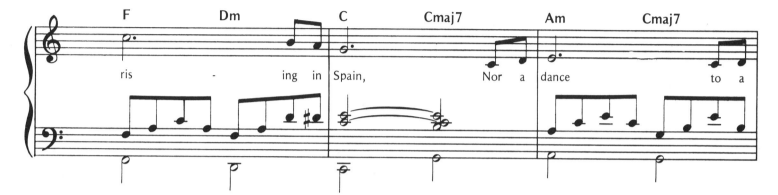

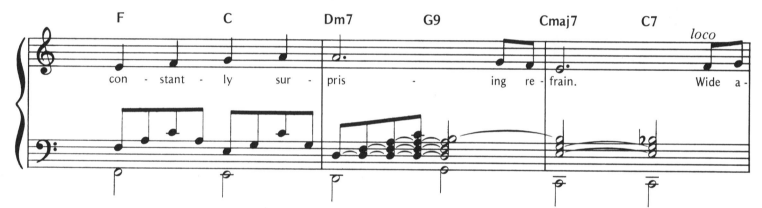

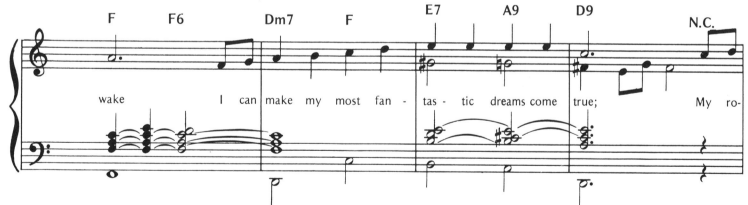

Red Roses for a Blue Lady

Electronic Organs
Upper: Flutes (or Tibias) 16′, 8′, 5-1/3′, 4′
       Add Percuss
Lower: Flutes 8′, 4′
Pedal: String Bass
Vib./Trem.: Off

Drawbar Organs
Upper: 83 6030 400
       Add Perc.
Lower: (00) 6402 003
Pedal: String Bass
Vib./Trem.: Off

Words and Music by Sid Tepper
and Roy C. Bennett

Light Swing beat (not fast)

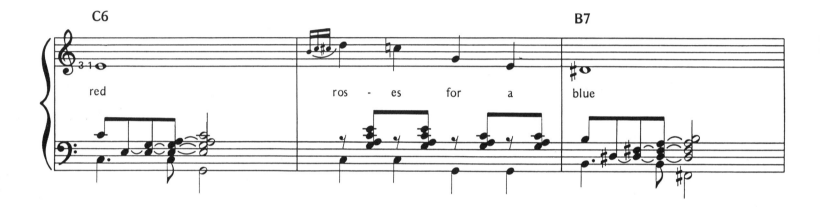

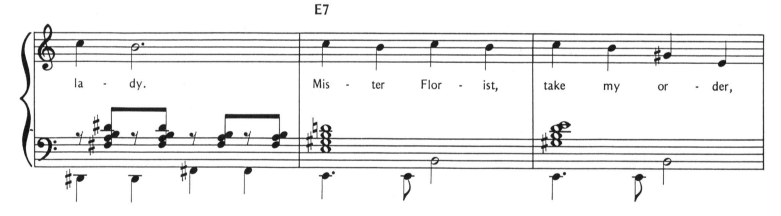

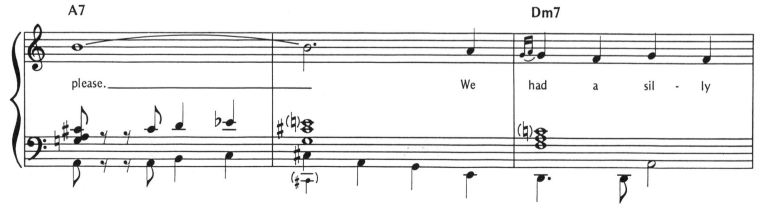

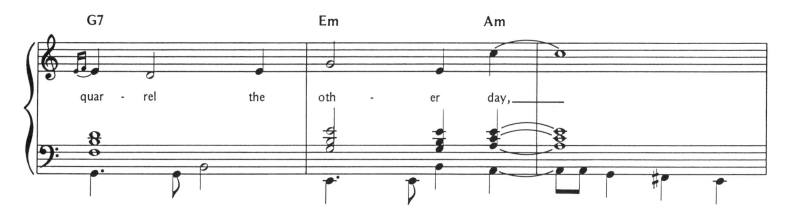

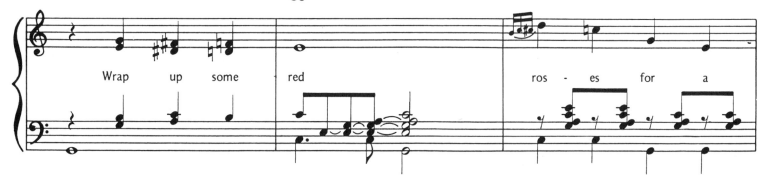

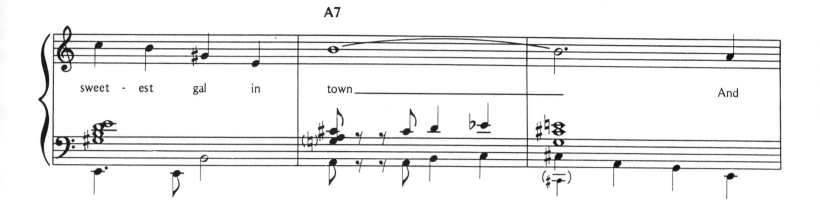

sweet - est gal in town _____ And

if they do the trick, I'll hur - ry back to

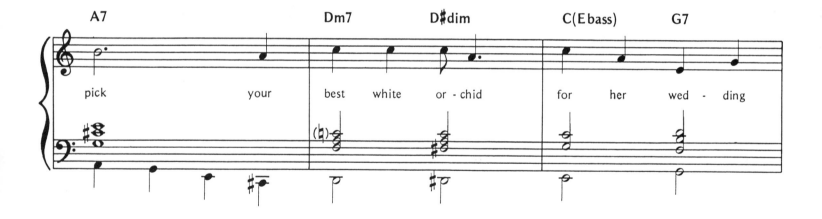

pick your best white or - chid for her wed - ding

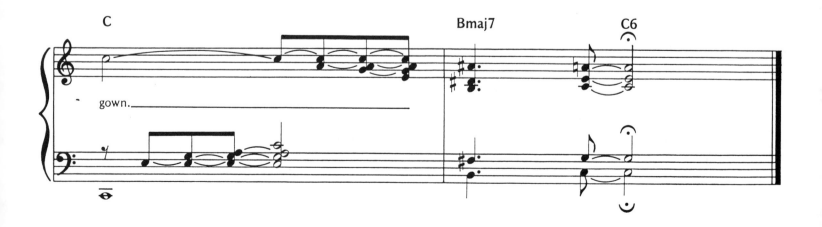

gown. _____

Some Enchanted Evening

from SOUTH PACIFIC

Electronic Organs
Upper: Flutes (or Tibias) 8', 4'
      String 8'
Lower: Flute 8'
      String 8'
Pedal: 8'
Vib./Trem.: On, Fast

Drawbar Organs
Upper: 20 7702 000
Lower: (00) 7503 000
Pedal: 04
Vib./Trem.: On, Fast

Lyrics by Oscar Hammerstein II
Music by Richard Rodgers

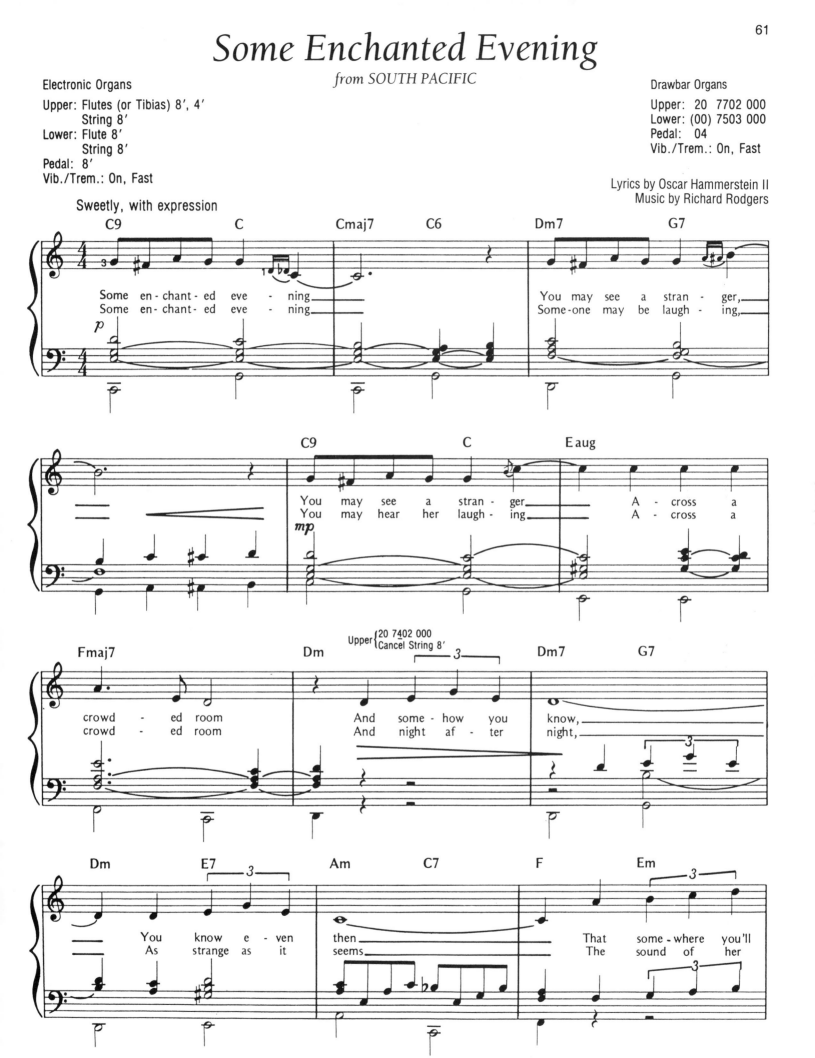

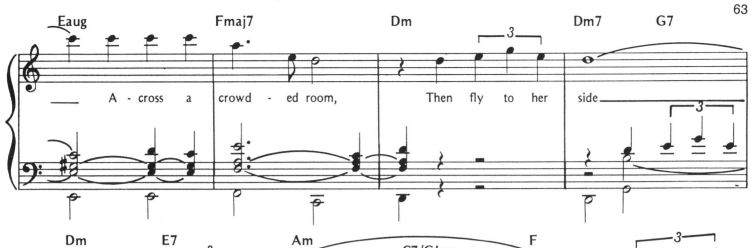

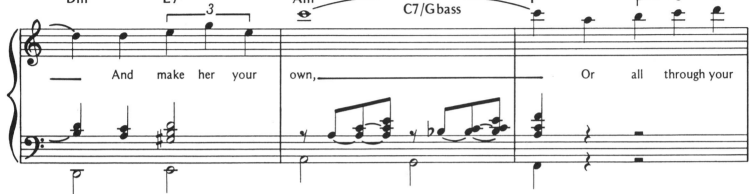

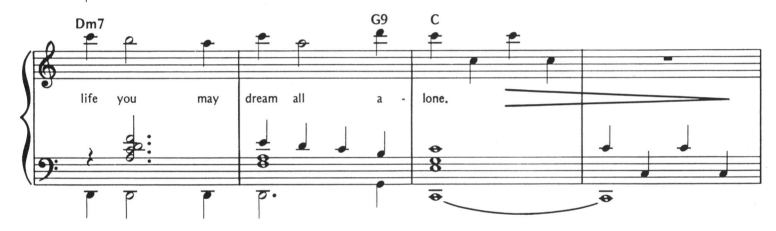

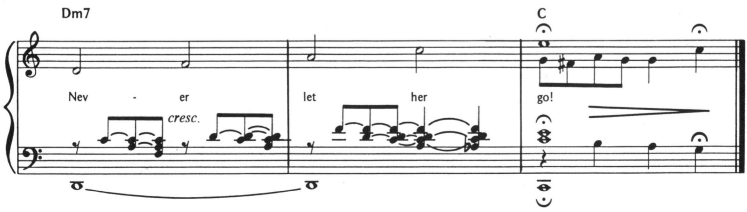

September Song
from the Musical Play KNICKERBOCKER HOLIDAY

Electronic Organs

Upper:	String 8', Flute (or Tibia) 4'
Lower:	String 8', Flute 8'
Pedal:	16', 8', Sustain
Vib./Trem:	On

Drawbar Organs

Upper:	04 8800 402
Lower:	(00) 5642 000
Pedal:	41, Sustain
Vib./Trem.:	On

Words by Maxwell Anderson
Music by Kurt Weill

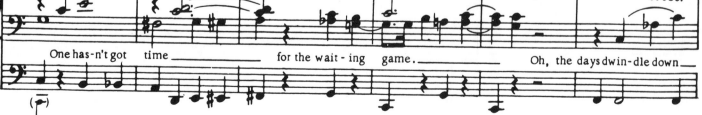

Slightly Out of Tune
(Desafinado)

Electronic Organs
Upper: Flutes (or Tibias) 16′, 8′, 4′, 2′
Lower: Flutes 8′, 4′, Diapason 8′
Pedal: String Bass
Vib./Trem.: On, Slow

Tonebar Organs
Upper: 80 6606 000
Lower: (00) 7400 000
Pedal: String Bass
Vib./Trem.: On, Slow

English Lyric by Jon Hendricks and Jessie Cavanaugh
Original Text by Newton Mendonca
Music by Antonio Carlos Jobim

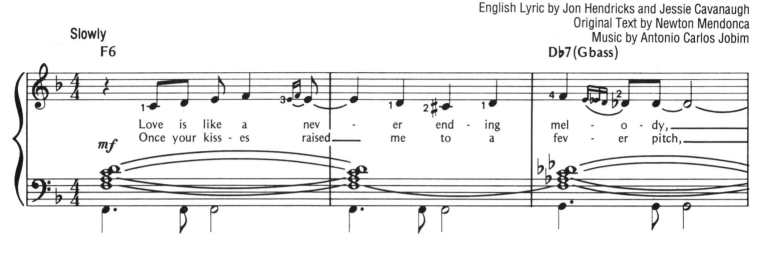

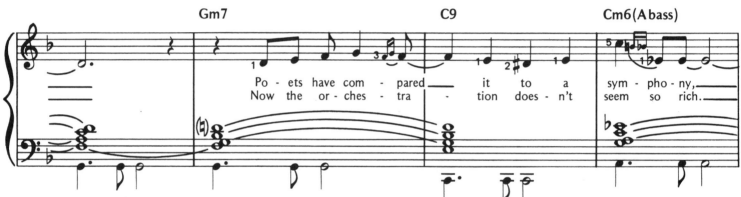

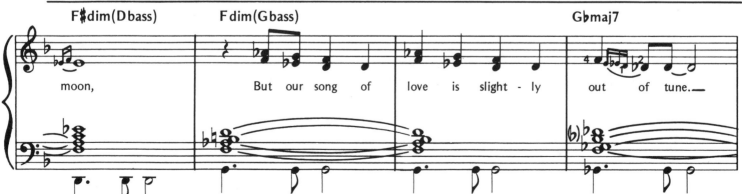

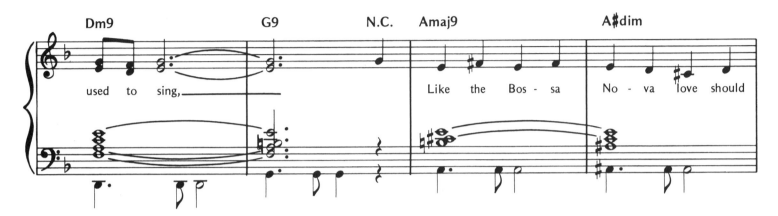

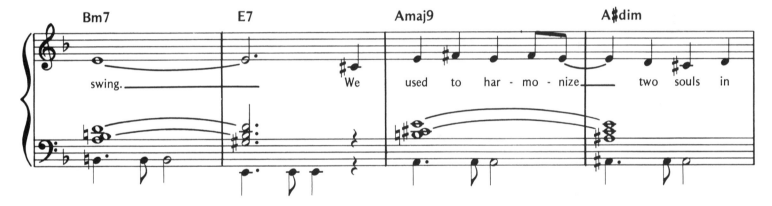

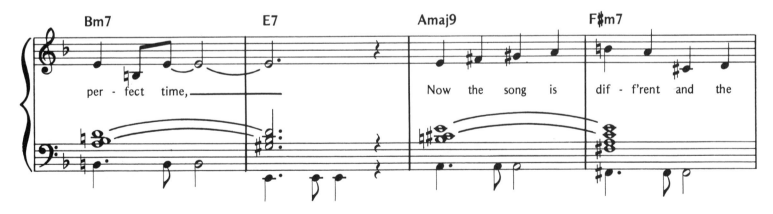

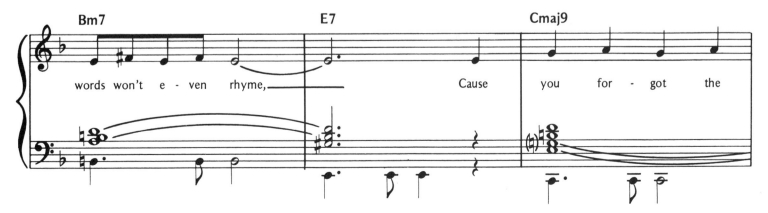

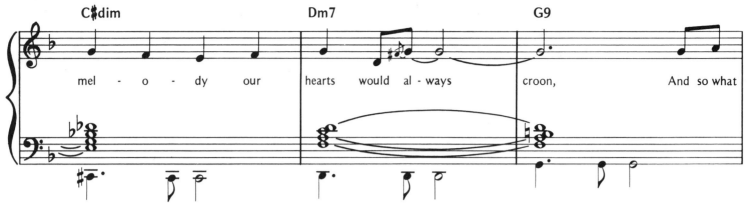

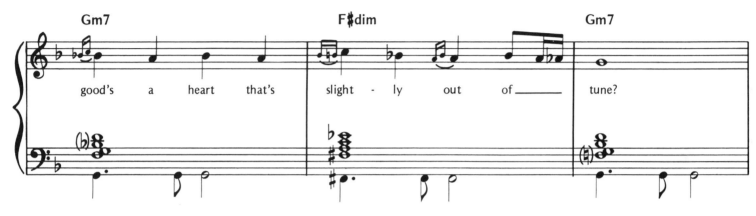

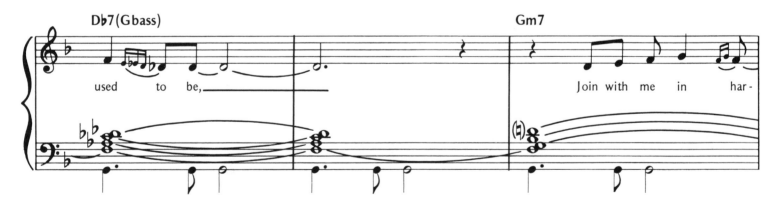

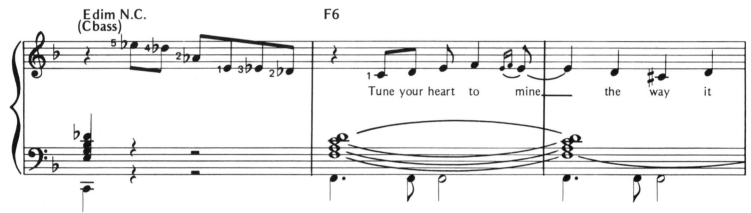

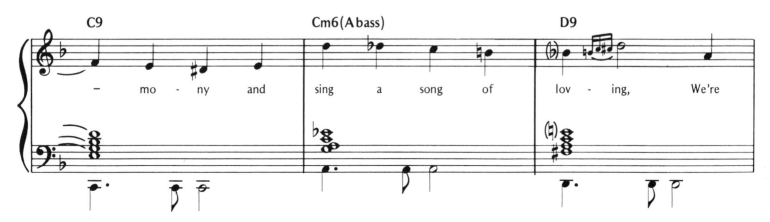

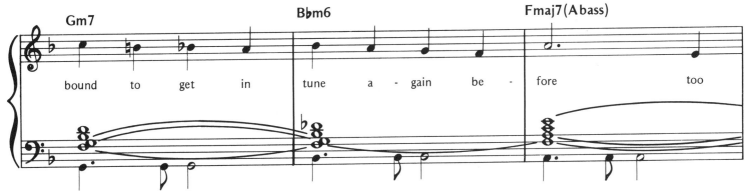

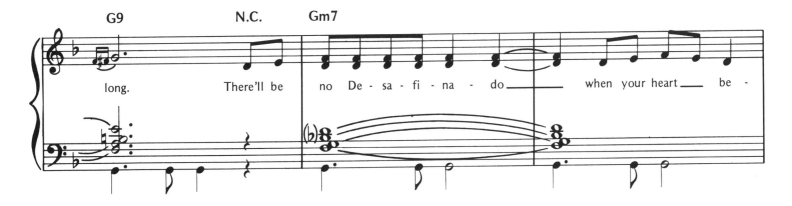

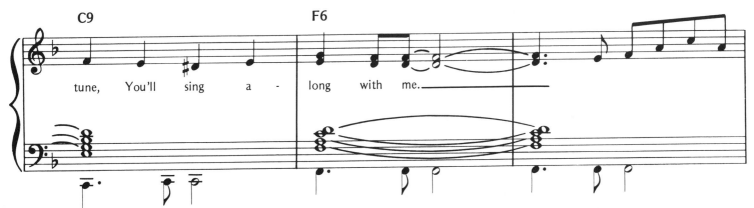

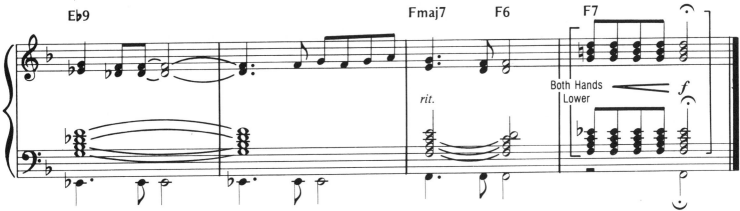

So Nice
(Summer Samba)

Electronic Organs

Upper: Flutes (or Tibias) 8', 4'
        Trumpet, Oboe
Lower: Flute 4', Diapason 8', String 8'
Pedal: String Bass
Vib./Trem.: On, Fast

Tonebar Organs

Upper: 88 0808 088
Lower: (00) 8648 003
Pedal: String Bass
Vib./Trem.: On, Fast

Original Words and Music by Marcos Valle
and Paulo Sergio Valle
English Words by Norman Gimbel

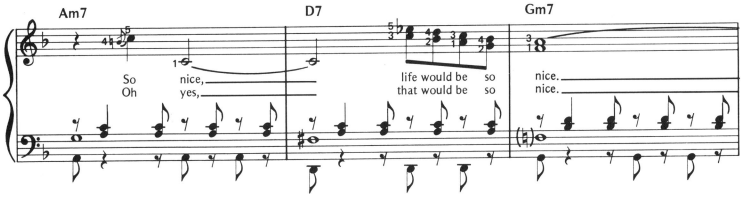

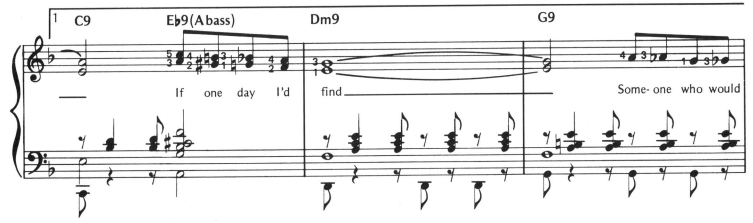

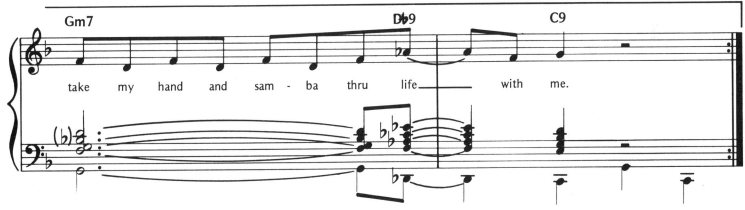

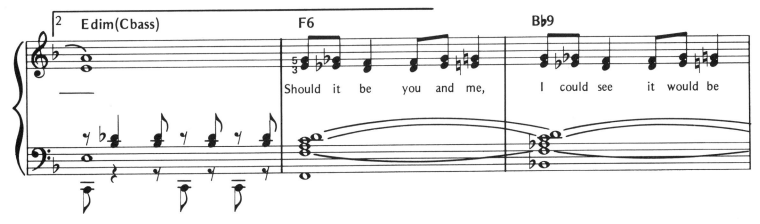

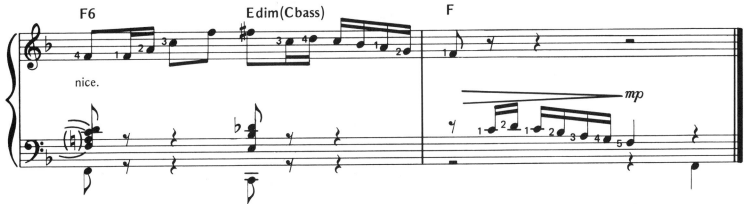

Watch What Happens

from THE UMBRELLAS OF CHERBOURG

Electronic Organs
Upper: Flutes 16', 8', 4', 2'
       String 8', Clarinet
Lower: Flute 8', Melodia 8',
       String 4'
Pedal: String Bass
Vib./Trem.: On, Fast

Tonebar Organs
Upper: 80 8104 103
Lower: (00) 8303 004
Pedal: String Bass
Vib./Trem.: On, Fast

Music by Michel Legrand
Original French Text by Jacques Demy
English Lyrics by Norman Gimbel

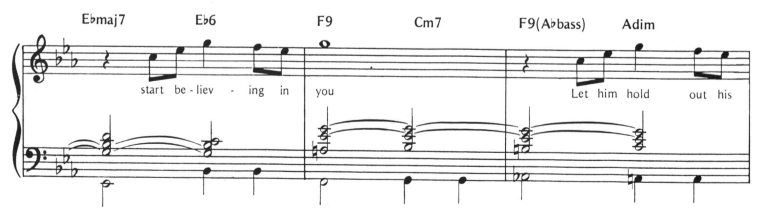

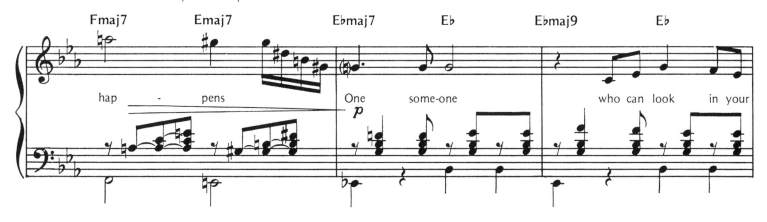

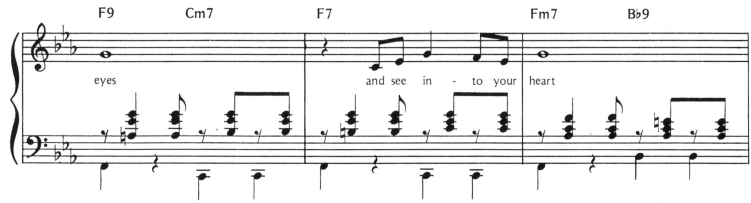

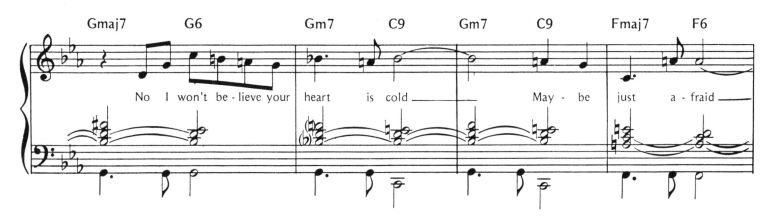

Younger Than Springtime

from SOUTH PACIFIC

Electronic Organs
Upper: Flutes (or Tibias) 16', 8', 4', 2'
       String 8', Clarinet
Lower: Flutes 8', 4'
Pedal: 16', 8'
Vib./Trem.: On, Fast

Drawbar Organs
Upper: 80 8104 103
Lower: (00) 7615 004
Pedal: 25
Vib./Trem.: On, Fast

Lyrics by Oscar Hammerstein II
Music by Richard Rodgers

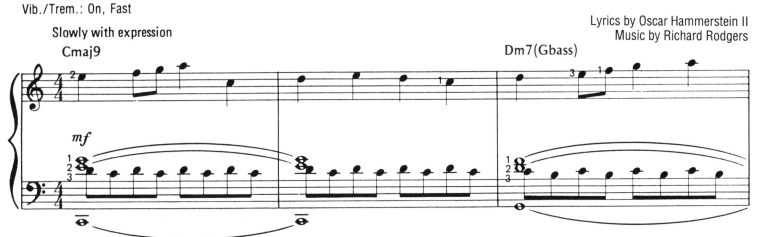

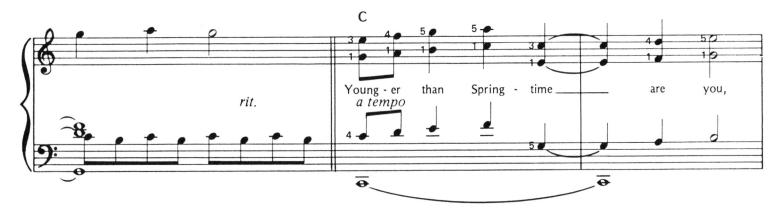

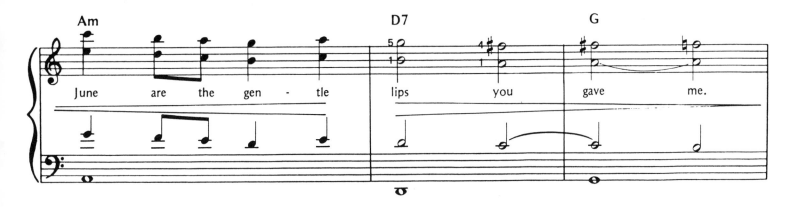

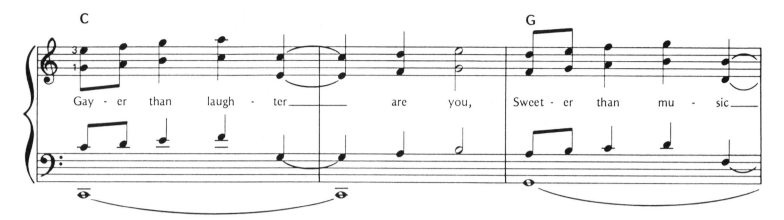

Gay - er than laugh - ter ___ are you, Sweet - er than mu - sic ___

___ are you, An - gel and lov - er, heav - en and earth are

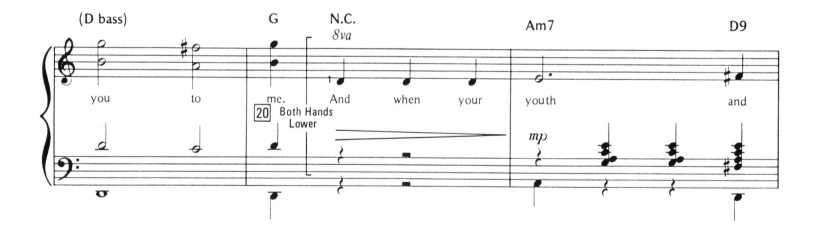

you to me. And when your youth and

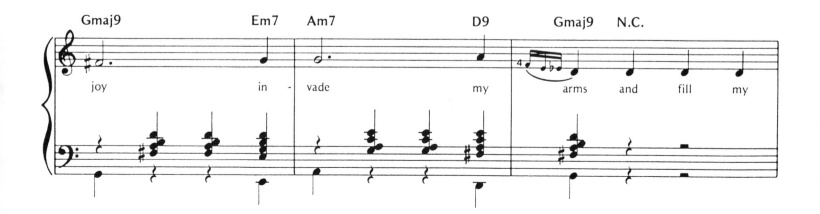

joy in - vade my arms and fill my

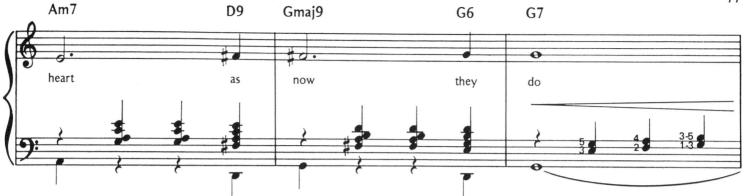

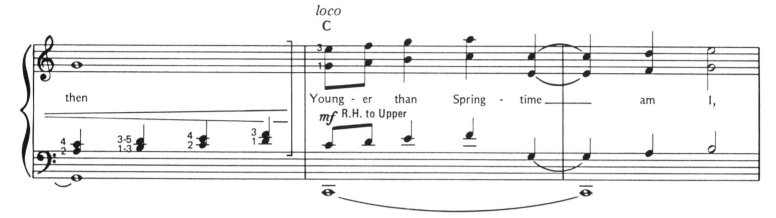

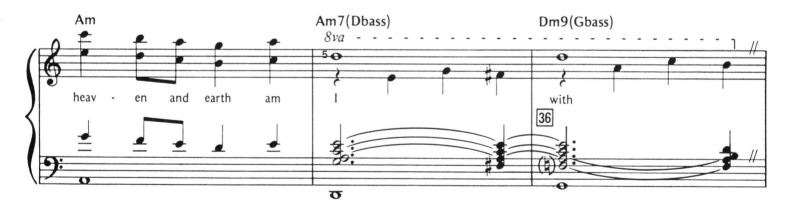

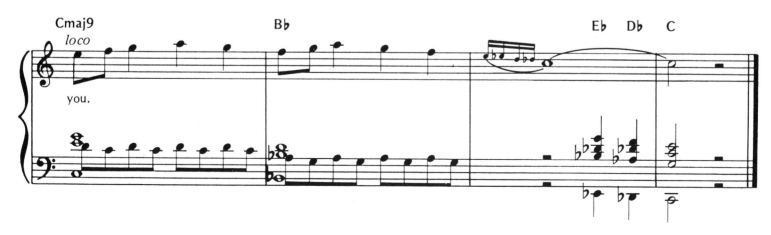